TYPE ADDICTED
THE NEW TREND OF A TO Z TYPO-GRAPHICS

Published and distributed in Europe by:

Index Book, SL
Consell de Cent, 160 local 3
08015 Barcelona, Spain
Phone: +34 93 454 5547
Fax: +34 93 454 8438
ib@indexbook.com
www.indexbook.com

Published and distributed for the rest of the world by

viction:ary™

viction:workshop ltd.
URL: www.victionary.com
Email: we@victionary.com

Edited and produced by viction:workshop limited
Foreword by Stefan Gandl, Neubau (NeubauBerlin.Com)

Book design by viction:design workshop
Concepts & art direction by Victor Cheung

©2007 viction:workshop ltd.
The copyright on the individual texts and design work is
held by the respective designers and contributors.

ISBN 978-84-96774-29-2

Acknowledgements
We would like to thank all the designers and companies
who made significant contribution to the compilation of
this book. Without them this project would not have been
possible.

We would also like to thank Stefan Gandl from Neubau
(NeubauBerlin.Com) for writing the foreword and all the
producers for their invaluable assistance throughout.
Its successful completion also owes a great deal to
many professionals in the creative industry who have
given us precious insights and comments. We are also
very grateful to many other people whose names do not
appear on the credits but have made specific input and
continuous support the whole time.

Future Editions
If you would like to contribute to the next edition of
Victionary, please email us your details to submit@
victionary.com

THE NEW TREND OF A TO Z
TYPO-GRAPHICS

TYPE ADDICT-ED

www.indexbook.com

Typography is the hybrid of type and graphics, which brings dull languages alive and makes the whole design shine on stage; yet it always stays at the last row, being neglected and ignored. You may pass over typography which does not refer only to the design of types, but also the play with words as well as the arrangement and appearance of different elements on 2-dimensional printed matters and 3-dimensional spatial design. Humans think and perceive everything that they can feel consciously: we see when images come into our eyes, we hear when sound waves reach our ears, and we feel when objects are rubbed on our flesh… but we always overlook what lies intrinsically.

Audiences always think that they are captivated by the fascinating graphics but they would never be aware of what really hooks them up with the message behind. Languages deliver messages that are what we cannot live without, though we are often fed up with languages. Sometimes we prefer going for movies rather than reading books. Children draw cartoons on their textbooks. Most of us seek visual impacts besides languages. Do you prefer reading from line to line of a passage like this for your whole life? Sure you don't although many of us immerse ourselves in the written world; we can never live without tedium in a pure-word world. Typographic elements convey messages and create a much stronger bombardment to audiences by creative arrangement and combination of languages with different graphic ornaments. Typography saves us from boredom. It visualizes languages in physical forms and makes the whole language world dazzle.

Different typefaces give different mood, and we should choose the proper one for different occasions. Remember when you type the job application letter, you use 'Times New Roman' or 'Arial' rather than 'Comic Sans MS' or 'Shorthand,' don't you? You play with funny handwritings and lovely symbols in letters for your best friends, and you write neatly when you have to drop your boss a line. Your kids love to have their names 'written' with different embellishment on the door of their rooms, showing the particular characters of their little domain. Everyone uses type with purposes; indeed one and all are unconsciously typographers.

Throughout human history, artists evoke audiences' attention by bringing memorable mood from the hybrid. Posters with eye-catching graphics and types can stay longer in your mind. Typography is the glare of publicity that spotlights identity and gives spirit to creative brands by integrating languages and visual collision, which ultimately reaches the finest stage of aspiration. The easiest recognizable examples are the definable typographic designs of different brand names. Typographers play an important role in establishing brand identity through the blending of brand images into types and the creation of distinctiveness. Let's grab a can of coke for example. The typographer of 'Coca-cola' did a brilliant job. One can easily recall the red Coca Cola package with its Spencerian script type which was developed in the mid-19th century. It was once a dominant form of handwriting in the United States, which presented a 'daily' and 'friendly' image to the brand and resulted in a huge success. In contrast, the largest competitor of Coca Cola, Pepsi, develops a totally different image in order to secure a place in the market. In 1991, the brand started to be in italic capital typeface which runs vertically up the blue package brings 'cool' and 'fashionable' perception and a triumph in the market.

Besides, typography helps storytellers give amazing stories everyday. It doesn't only refer to the typeface design but as well how we put everything together in the layout or space. Pick a magazine and flip. What makes you go through the lines – controversial headlines, creative graphics, or interesting layout with good pictures in attractive topic? Headlines or graphics may not make an editorial stand out of the crowd. Layout with graphics and words arranged wisely outstands the whole story. Like Sylvia Tournerie who designs layouts for the free contemporary art magazine '02,' she made very good examples through the arrangement of graphics and words which catches our eyeballs.

Typography does not survive only in the 2-dimensional world. Designers also tell stories by applying typography spatially. Oded Ezer suggests a playful and entertaining attitude in his work 'Tybrid' by releasing himself freely and intuitively, forming a Hebrew word 'Typography' in 3-dimensional context. Tsang Kin-wah integrates poem with great music by embedding typography in a stage design for the event 'Clavecin + Percussion III.' Typographic designs are like pillars of a stage where storytellers give their best stories.

The typographic world as well provides opportunities for designers to intermingle sundry cultures. By mixing languages with characters from different cultures and even religions, designers create a brand new stage of amazement. Milkxhake designers mesmerize everybody in the poster 'pray&pay' by combing Chinese traditional religious beliefs with English characters to show the relationship between God and human. With the words that made up of 'Yuen Bo,' a Chinese traditional paper money made for ancestor, designers wisely demonstrate the belief of traditional Chinese: people worship and contribute (in terms of money) in order to show respect and responsibility. Other than exhibition posters, typography on top walks into our daily lives with cultural and religious elements. Designers apply their talents in what we can come across everyday: signages, logos, calendars, T-shirts, you name it. Here comes a good example from Khaki Creative & Design, Inc. With more and more people come to the capital of China - Beijing, the designer welcomes prospective visitors with creative typographic tour by creating various logotypes 'Welcome to Bejing.' Sixstation in Hong Kong also did an excellent job in typographic T-shirt graphics. Commissioned by Atomicsushi, the talent expresses respect to the 60's Hong Kong film's fighting scene by combing visuals with the word 'Shaolin,' a mark of Chinese kung fu.

The digitalization of technology has helped typography rise to a new level too. Typesetters and designers no longer need to make up new types on drawing boards or with letterpress, and more possibilities appear with new technologies such as digital printing and filming. More types come into life with computerized effects and tones. Take a look at the different styles in the 'Safe As Milk Festival' created by the talents of Grandpeople. The designers fused Egyptology with psychedelic approach by printing types with gold folio embossment so as to focus on the festival's theme 'Money.' The designers grasped a totally different approach for the festival in the following year. With computerization, they came up with the stimulation of putting experimental music together with B-film horrible elements. The idea is used in the festival's promotional items and made all and sundry call to mind.

Over the pages, Type Addicted looks at the allure of type from different perspectives; from 2-dimensional designs on printed matters like album cover, poster, promotional material to 3-dimensional display, stage design and installation, type-addicts from all over the world inspire us with the wisdom of how they create new typefaces and how they deal with different types of fonts in the arrangement of layout; it certainly explores the new wave of typography. Artists like Atelier télescopique, Conor & David, Dainippon Type Organization and Neubau (NeubauBerlin.Com) will tour you around with the 26 alphabets; playful yet connotative, subtle yet rousing, each of those represents great works in the field, and delicates how creative languages can be made and evolved when they are assimilated in the horizon of typography.

INTRODUCTION

When being asked to do the foreword for this book and while considering its title 'Type Addicted,' I thought it would be helpful to start by defining the term 'type addiction.' In addition I would use myself as an example patient to define the nature of this sort of 'disease.'

Thanks to the digital age and the inventions of the revolutionary platform-independent page description language 'Post-Script,' the typographic virus has spread from a small group of very specialized individuals to a much larger group of specialists and non-specialists within the last 20 years.

The liberalization of technology and type-production tools made it possible for almost everyone – including myself – to be infected. And even though there are thousands of different digital typefaces available today, the demand for individual expression seems to be stronger than ever. 'Type Addicted' will help you keep an overview of the current global typographic 'epidemic.'

BUT WHAT IS 'TYPE ADDICTION?'

'Type addiction' could be described as a periodic compulsion to an individual (i.e.: a typographer, typesetter, graphic artist, designer, etc.) who occupied by the art and techniques of type design and its possibilities of glyphs-modifications and type arrangement.

GANDL'S ANAMNESIS STAGE 1

My personal anamnesis started very much unconsciously. In fact it could be compared to a kind of creeping 'infection' and perhaps it is important to foreclose that no matter what people say (like 'you're not talented,' 'stop it' etc.) it won't change your vicious habits once you are infected.

Although I really tried very hard, the teachers at elementary school weren't happy at all with my calligraphical output. I got bad marks on a regular basis. But that didn't stop me from what I was doing and I started drawing bold glyphs (characters) all over my notebooks. It got even worse during the 70s when I started to 'design' the covers of my own mix tapes myself. My pocket money wasn't sufficient to purchase the original records.

GANDL'S ANAMNESIS STAGE 2

Circa 79/80 a school friend gave me her Beatles single 'Help' on vinyl as a present. Unfortunately the cover jacket was missing so I needed to design it myself. My first typographical work for a record sleeve found me re-drawing all the modern grotesque characters by hand contained in the original record's sleeve-design.

During a time-consuming crisis and after the third black felt pen marker went out of business, I kind of successfully managed to combine cut-out imagery of black & white photocopy machines with my own drawings and rub-off typography.

GANDL'S ANAMNESIS STAGE 3

Unfortunately the result wasn't really that bad which gave me further confidence to go on experimenting with my new found toys – the dry transfer sheets of Letraset – which put my addiction to a new level.

Sadly enough these expensive sheets that were full of typography were available to me through one of my aunts who was an architect in those days.

GANDL'S ANAMNESIS STAGE 4

To cure me from type-infection, I was sent to Grafische Lehr – und Versuchsanstalt Wien 14 – a high school for applied graphic design in Vienna (Austria), which was a complete failure. The first few Apple Macs were available at school – a real revolution. These amazing computers were a temptation I couldn't resist and I buried my piles of Letraset sheets.

In order to safe us from total occupation by the disease we used these powerful tools for destroying existing typesets instead of creating new ones. Needless to say that it didn't help it.

GANDL'S ANAMNESIS STAGE 5

February 1992. I was tasked to digitize hand-drawn logos from the 60s and incorporate them into a corporate font. It was a final eye opener and my painful experience with Fontographer began.

At that time, the Fontographer manual was only available in English. It contained a lot of complicated terms that were indecipherable to me, yet my experiments with the software sparked off a new enthusiasm.

Internet and search engines weren't available in those days, so I was mainly following the trial-and-error method. Two weeks later, with a couple

of achievements and twice as many failures
under my belt, I was helplessly addicted to the
package. Ever since, I have worked on creating
programmed typography on a regular basis, while
my own handwriting gets worse and worse.

THERAPY

Typo-graphic and typography is an integrated
element of my profession - Special projects
require special typography. Still I wouldn't
consider myself a typographer but I definitely
dig into the experiment.

Over the years I developed some automatisms
with the available software in combination
with geometric forms that helps me producing
typefaces within some hours now. Usually I find
myself producing simple display typography that
has become more or less a necessary and playful
gymnastic for my system in order to keep my
body calm and relaxed.

The biggest problem to get cured is that
impossible to describe the feeling when you
install your own typeface on your computer and
see your glyphs running over the screen - letter
by letter, word by word, sentence by sentence
- for the very first time.

In order to prevent me from further damage I
started to produce letter stamps lately.

Boredom hasn't kicked in yet but eventually it
will help me by going back to the roots of my
addiction.

RECOMMENDATION

Unless you are of a particularly strong and
resilient constitution I recommend that you stop
reading here and cease reading this book or
accept the risk of 'infection' and perhaps of
becoming a type-addict too.

BY
STEFAN GANDL
NEUBAU
(NEUBAUBERLIN.COM)

{ths} Thomas Schostok
  Design
3 Deep Design
Adam Hayes
Alex Trochut
Andrew Byrom
Apirat Infahsaeng
artless Inc.
Artroom – Commercial
  Radio Productions
  Ltd.
Atelier télescopique
Build
Byggstudio
Claire Scully
CoDesign Ltd
Conor & David
Corp.Unit
Dainippon Type
  Organization
David Lane
desres design group
FromKtoJ/FromJtoK
gggrafik
Grandpeople
Guy Haviv
Gyöngy Laky
Hamlet Au-Yeung
HAWAII DESIGN London
Hjärta Smärta
Iceland Academy of
  the Arts, graphic
  design graduation
  class of 2006
Jo Ratcliffe
Khaki Creative &
  Design, Inc.
KOKOKUMARU,Co Ltd.
Lizzie Ridout
Made
Manuel Kiem
Michael Perry

Milkxhake
Misprinted Type
mylifesupport™
NB: Studio
Neubau
  (NeubauBerlin.Com)
Noa Bembibre
Non-Format
Oded Ezer Typography
Park Studio
Paulo Garcia/Lodma.
  Location Doesn't
  Matter Anymore
pleaseletmedesign
Post Typography
R2 design
Robert J.Bolesta
Serial Cut™
Si Scott Design
Siggi Orri
  Thorhannesson
Sixstation
Studio8 Design
Sylvia Tournerie
Taste Inc.
Tjep.
Tommy Li design
  Workshop Limited
Topos Graphics
Tsang Kin-wah
Vault49
Whaa
Widmest
Will Perrens
Wyeth Hansen
Yokoland
Zion Graphics

Key

T:title
D:design
P:photography
C:client
W:type of work
L:language
M:measurement
Y:year

A TO Z
TYPO-
GRAPHICS
PAGE
010 — 233

'Adult'

Poster announcing
Adult's performance.

T: Adult.
D: Apirat Infahsaeng in
   collaboration with
   Mary Banas
C: Bar for Adult.
W: Poster
L: English
Y: 2007

'Agility'

Agility type has been
created for the commu-
nication of an agility
dog contest. The idea
of the race is symbol-
ized by jumps, which
gives a 3-dimensional
effect to the type-
face.

T: Agility Typeface (Com
   munication for an
   Agility dog contest)
D: David Stettler (Whaa)
C: Ecal (University of
   Arts of Lausanne)
W: 3D typeface
L: French
Y: 2005

'Amazon'

A booklet and poster produced to raise awareness of the destruction of the Amazon rainforest for the US-based charity Rainforest Action Network (RAN). Copies of both the booklet and poster will soon be available at Magma bookshops, with all proceeds going to RAN. Each booklet is made from only 1 sheet of FSC certified paper, folding out from the cover into a 12-page concertina, maximizing the sheet and minimizing waste.

T:At This Rate
D:Studio8 Design
P:Giles Revell
C:Rainforest Action
  Network (RAN)
W:Editorial
L:English
Y:2007

Every day we lose an area larger than all five boroughs of New York City

5

3

Every year we lose an area three times the size of Sri Lanka

102

Every month we lose an area 102 times the size of Barcelona

'Amusement'

Cats Let Nothing
Darken Their Roar 2006
is a self promotional
calendar for the
designer's just
launched company. It
was intended to be
sent to friends and
colleagues on the
Christmas of 2005.
The idea was to create
an everyday tool
that would provoke,
surprise, shock and
amuse every month
throughout the year.

T: Cats Let Nothing
   Darken Their Roar
   2006
D: Noa Bembibre
C: Noa Bembibre
W: Calendar
L: English
Y: 2006

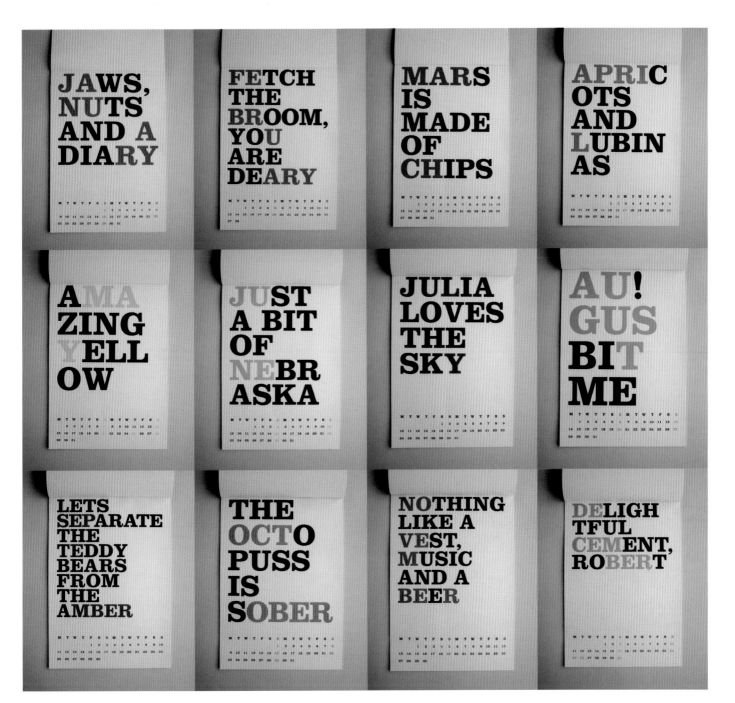

'Analogue'

NBGrotesqueNo9™ is the
headline typography of
the 'Remember/Revolver'
book project. The
project and typeface
are the collaboration
between the artist
and musician Klaus
Voormann (designer
of legendary Beatles
Revolver sleeve 1966)
and the designer Stefan
Gandl. NBGrotesqueNo9™
was designed on the
computer and later on
laser stenciled in
order to receive single
character stamps.
These character stamps
were used to fit with
the analogue feel of
the illustrations
within this project.

T: NBGrotesqueNo9™
D: Neubau
   (NeubauBerlin.com)
C: Voormann.com
W: Illustration,
   Promotion
L: English
Y: 2006

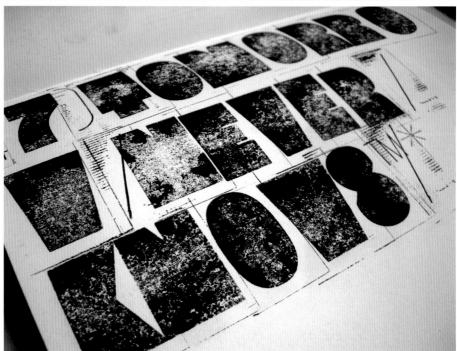

NB
GROTES
QUE™

ABCDEFGHIJK
LMNOPQRS
TOMORROW/N
EVER/KNOWS
UVWXYZ/0123
456789

'Anthology'

'Collecting Flowers,'
Oslo Architects
Association's spring
programme 2006, was
a series of lectures
with the subtitle
'An anthology of
Architecture and Art.'
The brief was to reflect
this theme, and to
make a poster design
dissimilar to the
designs traditionally
used in this context.

_____

T: Collecting Flowers
   – Spring
D: Grandpeople
C: Oslo Architects
   Association
W: Poster
L: Norwegian
Y: 2006

COLLECT ARCH FLOWERK

2.2
BAUMSCHLAGER
EBERLE ARCHITEKTEN
(Østerrike)
CHRISTIAN AUGUSTS GATE 23 / KL 19:00

18.2
DAN GRAHAM
(USA)
"OWN WORKS"
AHO, MARIDALSVEIEN 29 / NBI LØRDAG KL 13:00

9.3
TESTBED STUDIO
(Sverige)
OAF / KL 19:00

16.5
VAN BELLE &
MEDINA
(Belgia)
OAF / KL 19:00

30.3
DORTE MANDRUP
(Danmark)
OAF / KL 19:00

20.4–22.1
OCA CONFERENCE + ISMS
SE ANNONSERING FOR TESPUND

27.1
GENERALFORSAMLING

B-ARCHITECTEN
(Belgia)
OAF / KL 19:00

11.5
CH+QS
(Spania)
CHURTICHAGA - QUADRA SALCEDO ARQUITECTOS
OAF / KL 19:00

1.6
RICK JOY
(USA)
OAF / KL 19:00

9.6
SOMMERFEST
TID OG STED ANNONSERES SENERE. FØLG MED!

OSLO
ARKITEKTFORENING 100 ÅR
Våren 2006
EN ARKITEKTUR- OG KUNSTANTOLOGI

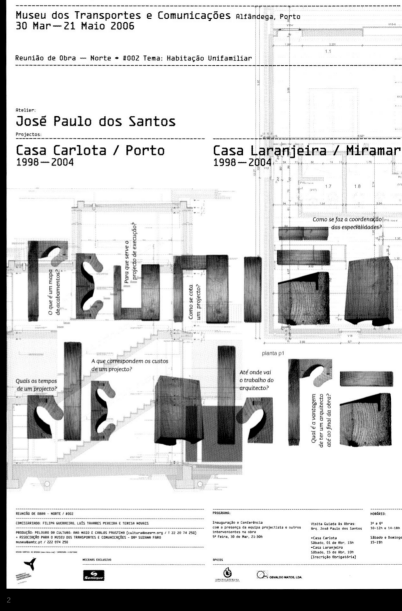

'Architecture'

Series of posters
for exhibition of
architecture aimed at
showing the public
the great importance
of the architect's
presence on site. Each
exhibition features a
Portuguese Architect.

T:1.Site meeting #04
  (Architect Siza
  Vieira)
  2.Site meeting #02
  (Architect João Paulo
  dos Santos)
D:R2 design

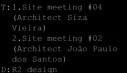

1

2

'Army'

Army theme of T-shirt design for Shanghai T-shirt store 'Shirt-Flag,' with the Chinese character '銃' (Chong) which is a kind of Chinese firemans.

_____

T:銃 (Chong)
D:Sixstation
C:Shirt-Flag
W:T-shirt graphic
L:Chinese
Y:2006

'Art'

T-shirt design for ChinaShadow. It is exhibited in Shanghai design biennial exhibition. This project event aims to promote and protect Chinese traditional art - shadow puppet.

T:一人唱盡天下事，
  雙手對舞百萬軍
  (ChinaShadow)
D:Sixstation
C:ChinaShadow
W:T-shirt graphic
L:Chinese
Y:2006

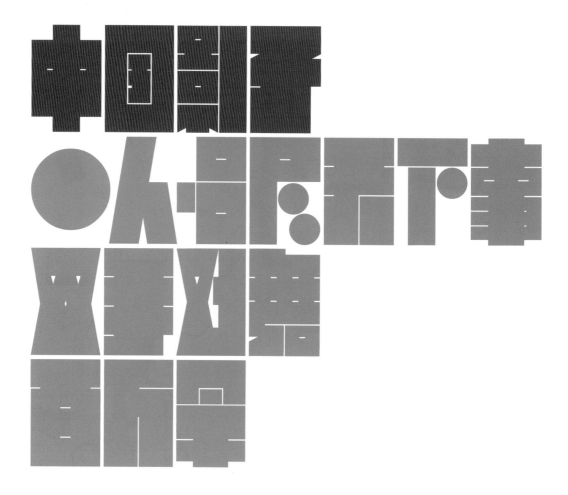

'Band'

3 different style logo designs for Singapore indie band 'Wu Feng Ling.'

T:Wufengling
D:Sixstation
C:Wu Feng Ling
W:Logo
L:Chinese
Y:2006

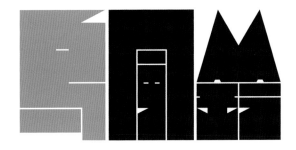

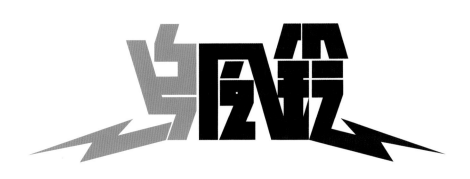

'Base'

Poster and visual
identity for
Contemporary Dance
Company HVDZ, Base 11-
19 show.

T: Base 11-19
D: Atelier télescopique
C: Cie Guy Alloucherie,
   Culture Commune
W: Poster
L: French
Y: 2006

'Basketball'

Type development for
the launch of LeBron
James's new basketball
shoe Zoom LeBron III.
Art direction by
Michael Spoljaric at
Nike Brand Design.

T: LeBron James, Zoom
   LeBron III
D: Non-Format
C: Nike
W: Typeface
L: English
Y: 2005

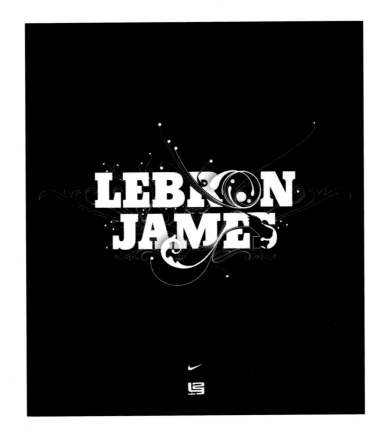

'Beijing'

Beijing is an up-and-coming city with too much flavour not to share with the rest of the world. Given that more and more people are coming to the city, many of whom might be in need of a suggestion or two, the designer thought he might provide a short typographical tour for any prospective visitor.

T:Welcome to Beijing!
D:Khaki Creative & Design, Inc.
C:Khaki Creative & Design, Inc.
W:Logotype
L:Chinese
Y:2007

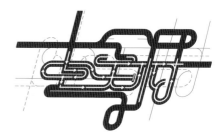

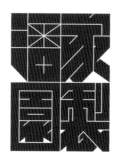

'Black'

The brief was to create a personal statement under the theme 'Black.' The statement was to portray the influence of the black colour when applied to graphics.

T: Everything Looks
   Better in Black
D: Paulo Garcia/Lodma.
   Location Doesn't
   Matter Anymore
C: Revista Colectiva,
   Costa Rica
W: Poster, Flyer
L: English
Y: 2007

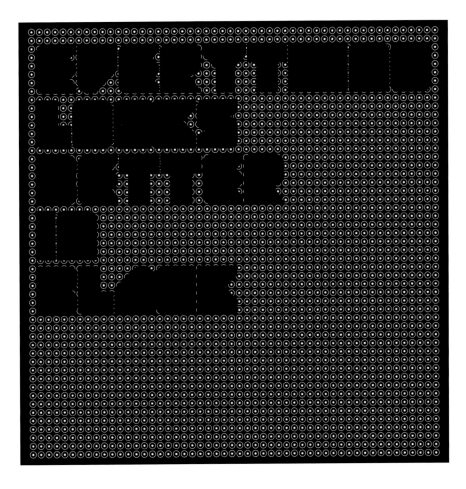

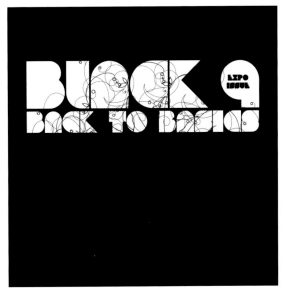

'Blending'

Portmanteau words come from blending 2 existing words into a new one. So this is the result: 6 strange blocked words in different typography at backlight.

T: Portmanteau
D: Serial Cut™
C: Perplex City
   (MindCandy)
W: 3D Typeface
L: English
Y: 2006

'Blocks'

Set of hand-painted
wooden letter block
loosely inspired by
children's alphabet
blocks. Instead of
being cubes, these
blocks are rectangu
and feature 3 diffe
styles of lettering

T:Alphabet Blocks
D:Post Typography
C:Post Typography
W:Hand-painted lette
   blocks
L:English
Y:2004

'Book'

1.The Bygg Books font (photographed real books) is a further experiment of the Book Club font using real books stacked on each other to form the letters of the alphabet.

2.The Book Club font (vector) was originally made as a school project for a literary dictionary. The book is about books, and the font is made by books itself. The idea is simple – to clearly communicate the content of the book and at the same time make it look a bit less heavy and more playfully pleasant than those kind of books normally do.

T:1.Bygg Books Font
  2.Book Club Font
D:Byggstudio
C:Byggstudio
W:Typeface
Y:2006

1

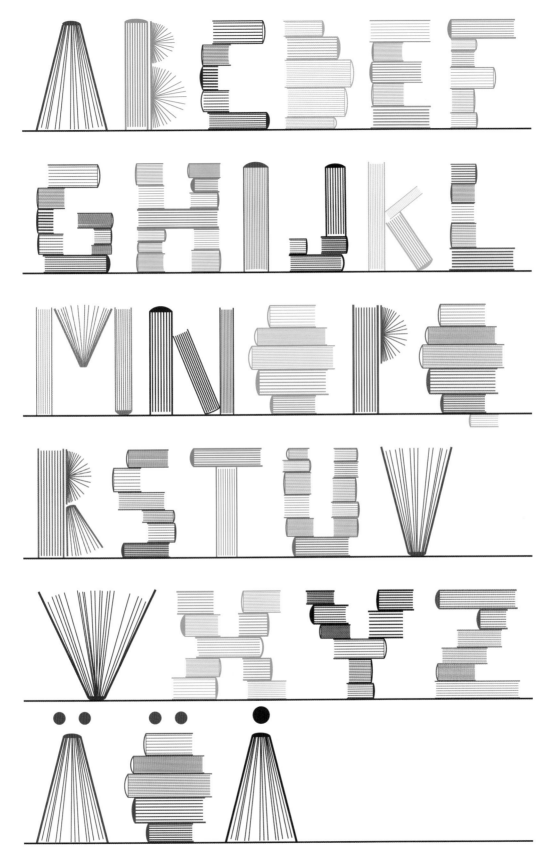

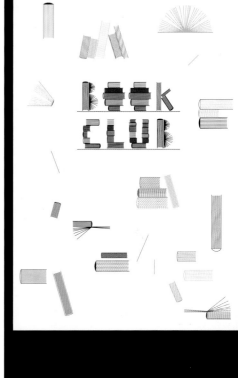

'Borderline'

Poster and visual
identity for Borderline
Festival 2004.

T: Borderline
D: Atelier télescopique
C: le Manège – Maubeuge
   (fr)/Mons (be)
W: Poster
L: French
Y: 2004

'Circuit'

To present the
different activities
of this association,
the designers decided
to make a big poster,
folded into a small
flyer. They like
the idea of people
unfolding it in the
middle of a concert
area.

T:Court Circuit
D:pleaseletmedesign
C:Court Circuit
W:Poster, Flyer
L:French
Y:2006

'Collage'

The designers asked a simple question on 'how do you express the scope and energy of the Channel 4 network?' when Channel 4 asked the studio to present their best stories of the year. The designers suggested taking the entire Review online, allowing people watch the programmes so as to create noise. Supported by a print version, the online Review succeeds in reflecting the diversity and energy of the Channel 4 network. Punctuated with small video screens, the site allows viewers to watch short clips of the biggest stories from 2006 with small screens set within collage frameworks comprising real objects and cardboard models representing specific programmes and campaigns. Constructed by hand, the collages suggest the creative flair of the network, providing an engaging, witty backdrop for the screens.

T: Channel 4 Annual
   Report
D: NB: Studio
C: Channel 4
W: Annual report,
   Poster, Online
   application
L: English
Y: 2007

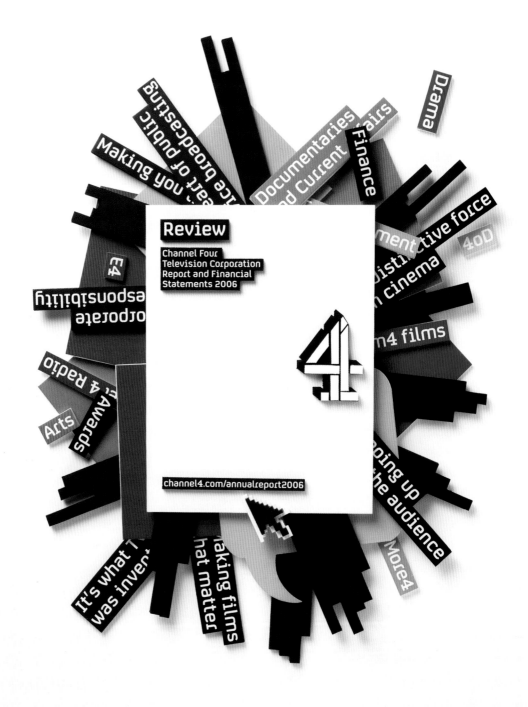

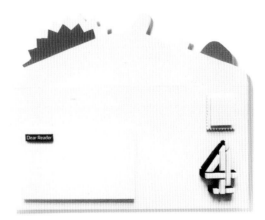

'Contacta'

Invitation card of
an exhibition for
the photographer
Bisse. The text is
silverfoiled on rough
brown cardboard. The
font used is a modified
Contacta.

T:Bisse
D:Zion Graphics
C:Bisse Bengtsson
W:Invitation card
L:English
Y:2005

'Creation'

The custom-made book cover was orginated from the motif of the creation of Chinese characters.

T: Book Cover Exhibition
D: Taste Inc.
C: Japan Typography
   Association
W: Custom-made Japanese
   Font
L: Japanese
Y: 2006

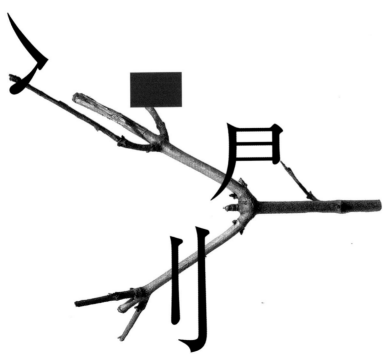

'Cube'

A divided cube
consists of 16 sides
with different signs
on each section. By
using these signs in
variable combinations
the whole alphabet
can be generated.
The prototype of
this cube can be
used as a 'writing
tool' for stamping
letters on paper or
on other surfaces.
The functional medium
is inspired by the
relevance of multiple
cases and repetitions
in everyday life.

T:Typecube
D:Manuel Kiem
C:Manuel Kiem
W:Experimental
  typography
Y:2006

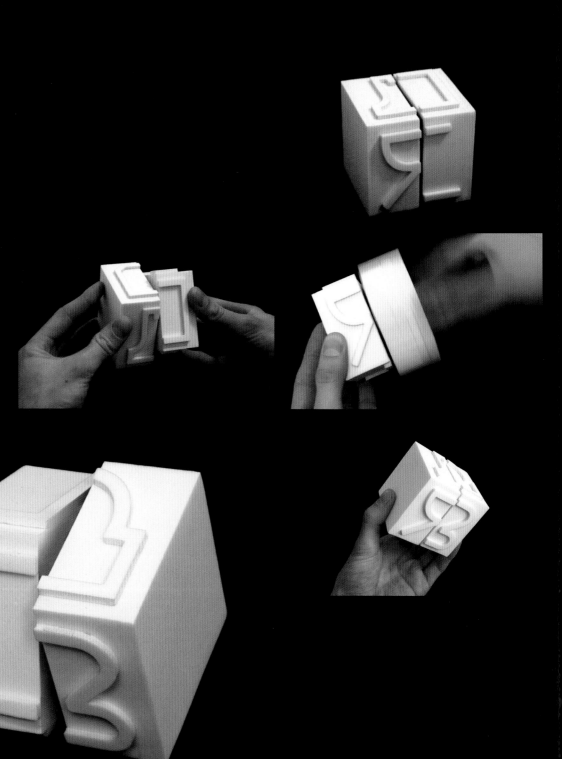

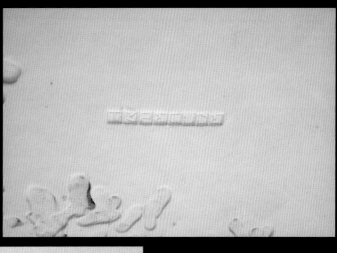

'Drawing'

Typeface made from
random drawings.

_____

T:Drawing Typeface
D:Michael Perry
C:Michael Perry
W:Typeface
L:English
Y:2003

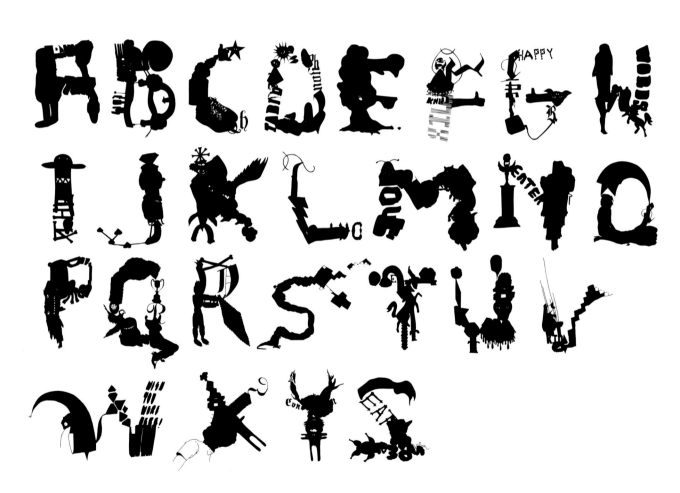

'Dream'

It was the ambition
in 2004 which means
'conquer the world.'

T:Dream
D:Dainippon Type
   Organization
C:RELAX Magazine
W:Editorial
L:Japanese
Y:2004

'Drift'

Concept for a display
font.

_____

T: Drift
D: Will Perrens
C: Will Perrens
W: logotype
L: English
Y: 2004

'Earring'

A typeface made of earrings. The design-ers use it for their own graphic identity.

T:Earring typeface
D:Hjärta Smärta
C:Hjärta Smärta
W:Typeface
L:English
Y:2004

'Editorial'

'Environment'

CO2 problem is a major problem for the ecology of the Earth. The typography on the wall surface expresses that CO2 problem and ecology are the same when it is viewed from a regular place. The typography is designed on the wall surface so as to materialize 2-dimensional typography in 3-dimensional space.

T:ECO2
D:KOKOKUMARU,Co Ltd.
C:Osaka University
  of Art
W:Typeface - DIN
L:English
Y:2005

'Etymology'

Self-initiated
typographic poster
celebrating the
etymology and form of
the ampersand.

T:&
D:Conor & David
C:Conor & David
W:Installation, Poster
L:English, Gaeilge
Y:2006

'Eyes'

This shirt design functions as both an abstract geometric pattern as well as clever cultural reference, thanks to the fragmented nature of the typeface. The phrase reads 'Les Yeux Sans Visage' which means 'Eyes Without A Face' in French, a reference to both the classic film of the same name and the Billy Idol song which followed. More directly, the phrase extends from the concept of the type 'face' which is purposefully incomplete, mirroring the 'face' in the phrase.

T: Eyes Without A Face
D: Wyeth Hansen
C: 2K By Gingham
W: T-shirt graphic
L: English, French
Y: 2006

'Fadar'

A typographic
interpretation of the
lyrics for 'Where Are
They Now' by Nas.

T:Where Are They Now?
D:Non-Format
C:The Fader
W:Editorial
L:English
Y:2006

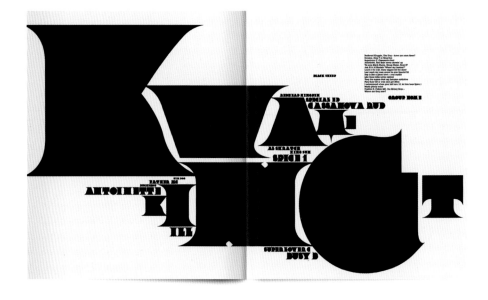

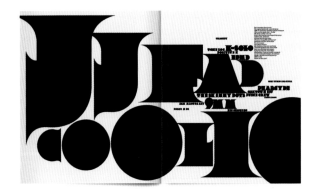

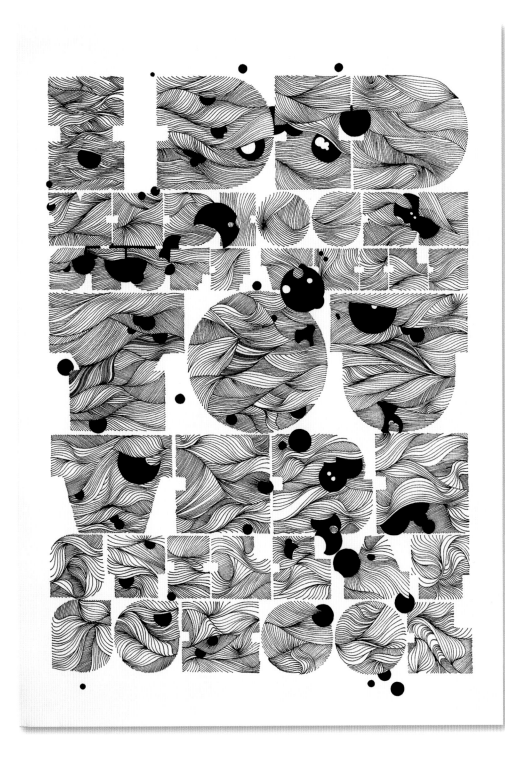

'Felt-tip'

Hand drawn poster for
Grafik Magazine's Felt-
Tip exhibition.

T: I Did Mediocre Stuff
   While You Were Still
   At School
D: Non-Format
C: Letraset, Grafik
   Magazine
W: Poster
L: English
Y: 2006

'Festival'

Safe As Milk is an annual festival for experimental music. In 2007 the designers used tools as a reference to proletarian propaganda iconography, in an effort to establish a connection to B-film horror movies and mysticism. These imagery stems from the obscure notion of Safe As Milk as a developing 'state within a state.' As the one in 2006 referred to currency, the designers revolves around ideology and state religion in 2007.

T:Safe As Milk #9
D:Grandpeople
P:Magne Sandnes
C:Safe as Milk Festival
W:Promotion
Y:2007

'Fifty'

A poster for a Swiss poster contest, concerning the 50th anniversary of the Swiss font Helvetica. For the designer, Helvetica is not bad and also not good. In German speaking countries, '0815' means standard or regular, it is not really top stuff.

T: 50 0815
D: gggrafik
C: gggrafik
W: Poster
L: German
Y: 2007

'Film'

Proposed visual
identity, posters, and
banners celebrating the
5th anniversary of the
Tribeca Film Festival
in New York City.

T: Tribeca Film Festival
   5th Anniversary
   (Unused)
D: Apirat Infahsaeng
C: Tribeca Film Festival
W: Visual identity,
   Poster, Banner
L: English
Y: 2006

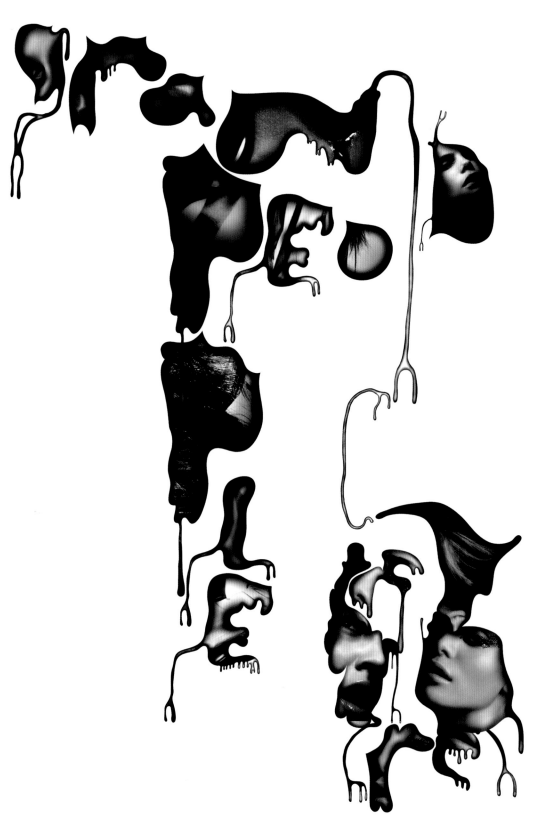

'Folklore'

AOI's new magazine 'Varoom' was launched on the 11th of May with a party and exhibition in London. Among Ed Fella, Genevieve Gauckler and others, Grandpeople contributed with 2 custom-made posters for this event. The posters have forms taken from Norwegian nature and folklore.

T: Grandpeople's
   Typography Troll
D: Grandpeople
C: AOI, Varoom Magazine,
   Grandpeople
W: Poster
Y: 2006

'French'

Poster and visual
identity for La Noche
Music Festival 2004.

————————————

T: La Noche
D: Atelier télescopique
C: RIF Association
W: Poster
L: French
Y: 2004

'Freezer'

In summer, the Freezer
DJ sets were spread out
over 3 days, so a 3-
dimensional typography
solution transmitted
this idea clearly:
Freezer Starts,
Freezer Fresh and
Freezer Finale! were
represented by a huge
type block based on
the Avantgarde font.

T:Triple Freeze
D:Serial Cut™
C:Freezer Morning Club
W:3D typeface
L:English
Y:2006

'Funky'

This is a promotional poster for a US street fashion store based in Hong Kong. Milkxhake took a funky and bold approach and developed a tailor-made typeface as the key visual for the launching poster.

T:The Studio by Pro Wolf
  Master
D:Milkxhake
C:The Studio by Pro Wolf
  Master
W:Poster
L:English
Y:2006

'Fuss'

Non-Format's 2006
exhibition 'Make A
Fuss' at Vallery
Gallery, Barcelona,
Spain.

T:Make A Fuss
D:Non-Format
C:Vallery Gallery
W:Poster
L:English
Y:2006

'G'

Designer's drawing on
the letter G.

T:The Letter G
D:Michael Perry
C:Michael Perry
W:3D typeface
L:English
Y:2006

'Game'

A collection of 8 hand-painted ceramic dishes for the book and exhibition 'Game Paused: A Creative Celebration of the Videogame.' For a project on this theme you could imagine pixels, LED screens and joysticks, but this aesthetic can also be represented in more organic ways. Pac-Man, Mario Bros, Donkey Kong, PaperBoy, Bubble Bobble and Sonic. The dishes can be used as collector pieces. Vector based first, hand-painted after, the Retro Game Icons are the traditional vision of the most memorable heroes.

T: Retro Game Icons
D: Serial Cut™
C: Game Paused
W: Ceramic
L: English
Y: 2006

designers to focus on
money for the festival,
so they used currency
as a thematic approach
for the visual profile.
Amongst the promotion
material was a single
colour bank note with
gold folio embossment
to ensure authenticity.
The visual profile
derived from a mixture
of Egyptology and
psychedelic.

———————————————————

T:Safe as Milk #8
D:Grandpeople
C:Safe as Milk Festival
W:Promotion
Y:2006

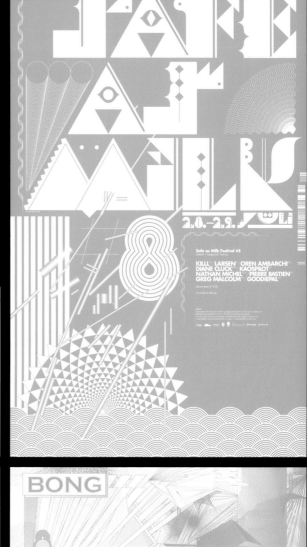

'Grab'

The initial idea for 'Grab-Me' came from studying the design of stencil letters. This developed into a 3-dimensional (low-relief) version that kept the breaks/support bars needed in a paper stencil. The breaks in a stencil design adhere almost perfectly made for the wall brackets needed in bathroom grab bars. The finished handrails are intended to make for the use in swimming pools or bathrooms.

T: Grab-Me
D: Andrew Byrom
C: Andrew Byrom
W: 3D typeface,
   Hand-rail design
L: English
Y: 2006

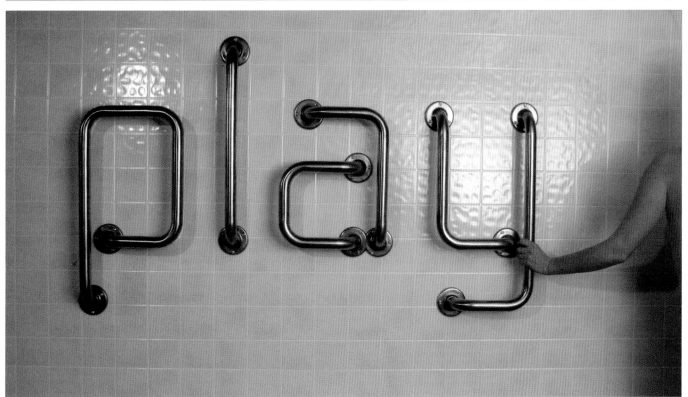

'Graduate'

Catalogue designed for
the Fashion & Textiles
graduates at the
University of Brighton.

T: Fashion & Textiles
   Catalogue
D: Will Perrens
C: University of
   Brighton Fashion &
   Textiles Graduates
   2006
W: Brochure design
L: English
Y: 2006

Mind block was created from an old pscoca-nalytical block game. There are 6 elements that can be used to create patterns. After some experiments the designer found that a 6x2 grid worked best and allowed a whole up-percase alphabet. The blocks were scanned and bitmapped.

T:Mind Block
D:David Lane
C:David Lane
W:Font design
L:English
Y:2006

MIND BLOCK CAPS/

TYPE FACE MADE US-ING BLOCKS FROM A PSYCHOLOGY TEST/

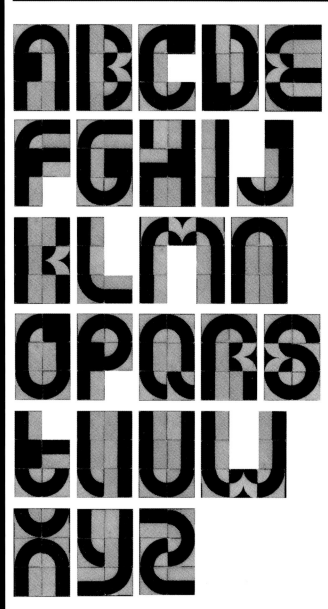

Each of the six sides of the blocks has a different pattern. When all the blocks are arranged on the same side a complete pattern is produced.
This caps alphabet is made up using four of the six sides/patterns that were available

The original set was produced by the National Founda-tion of Educational Research uk and The Psychogical Corperation, New York.

'Hand-drawn'

All work submitted was
part of a personal
project to create
illustrative fonts
from the standpoint of
an illustrator.

T:1,2.Experimental
  photographic Font
  3.Leaf Font
  4.Trunk Font
D:Claire Scully
C:Claire Scully
W:Hand-drawn typeface
L:English
Y:2007

1

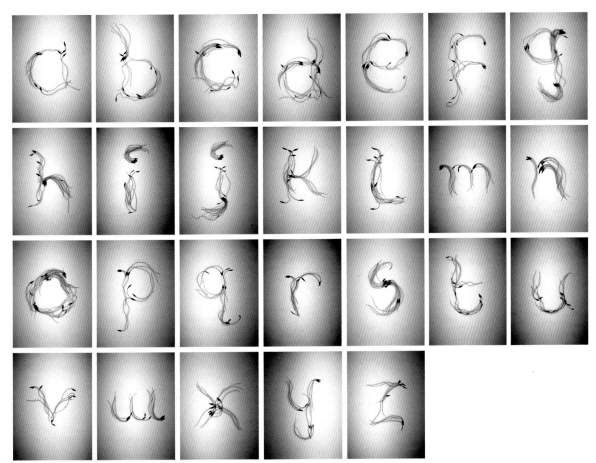

2

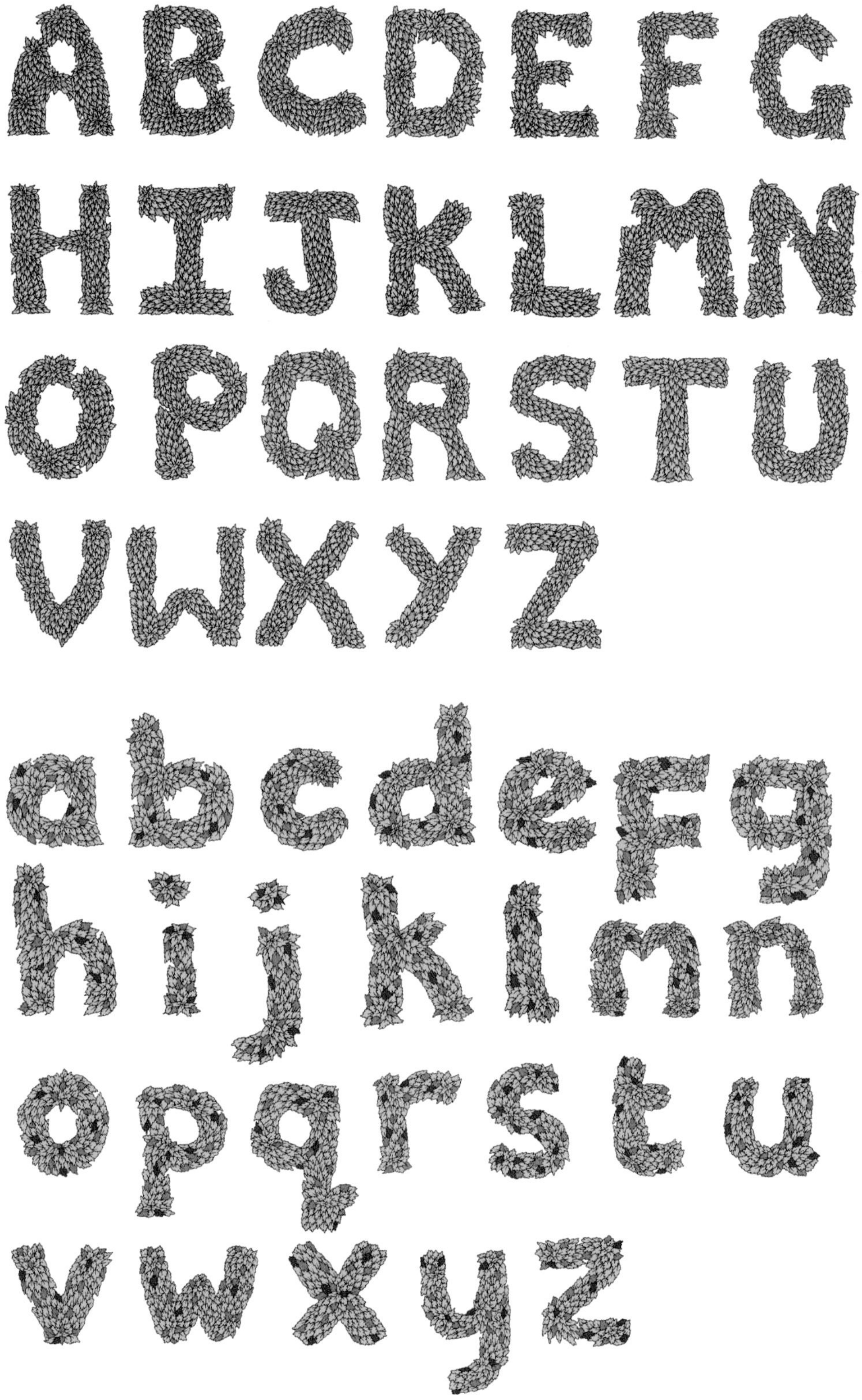

ABCDEFG
HIJKLMN
OPQRSTU
VWXYZ

abcdefg
hijklmn
opqrstu
vwxyz

4

'Help'

The 'Designed To Help'
project was launched by
UK designers iLovedust.
The idea was to produce
a book of graphic
design, illustration
and photography; and
to raise money for
charities that deal
with the tsunami crisis
in Asia.

T:A book Designed
  To Help
D:Atelier télescopique
C:DGV
W:Book Cover
L:English
Y:2005

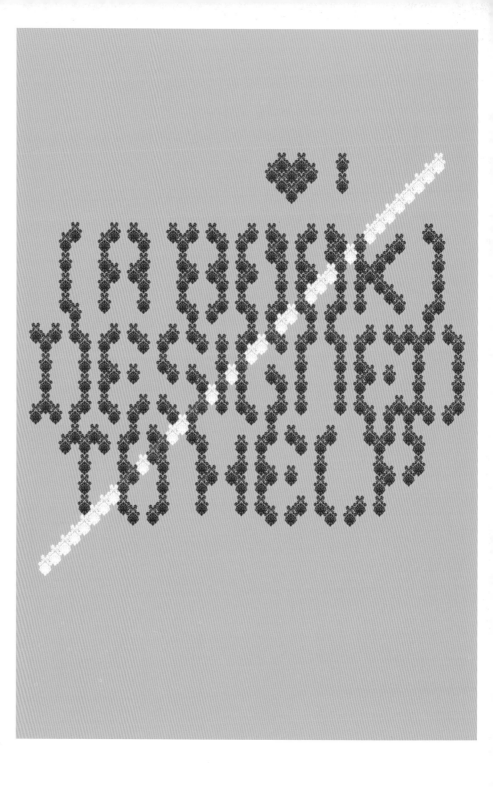

bank's 'O' logo, and
those are all recipes
for cookies – the most
universally relevant
language for the
holidays. The paper
acts as a kind of
window where the flakes
gather on the Happy
Holidays glass, and
the other side (the
inside) sports 'Warm
Wishes' and kitchen-
esque sentimentality.

_____

T:Warm Wishes!
D:Topos Graphics
C:Columbus Bank and
   Trust Co.
W:Holiday Card
L:English
Y:2006

'Home'

For an art exhibition
with the theme and
title 'HOME,' the
designer rearranged a
wall of bookshelves
in his apartment to
spell the word 'HOME.'
This photo was used on
invitations, postcards
and promotional
materials.

———————————————

T:HOME
D:Post Typography
C:Nancy Froehlich
W:Lettering
L:English
Y:2006

'I'

Poster design for 'Hompage to Helvetica Exhibition.' It is an exhibition in the new shopping mall 'Cantonyama.' In this project the designer was invited to create alphabet Helvetica 'i.'

T: I
D: Sixstation
C: Cantonyama
W: Poster
L: Chinese
Y: 2005

'Ice'

Christmas and New
Year card designed
with a custom-made
typeface inspired by
ice cubes and gift
box. An examination of
readability.

T: Seasons Greetings
D: Hamlet Au-Yeung
C: Hamlet Au-Yeung
W: Promotion
L: English
Y: 2006

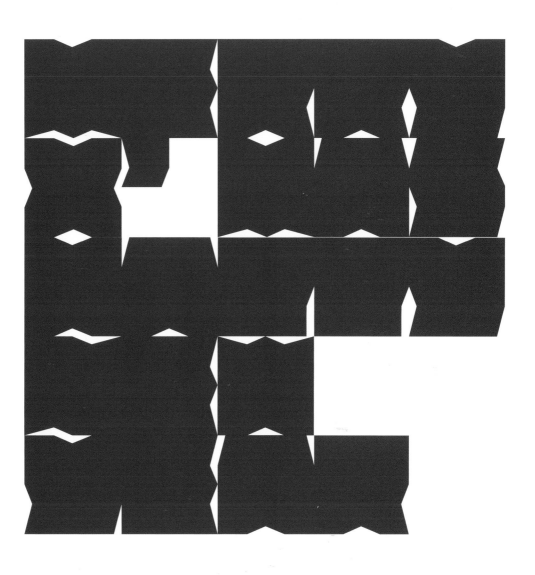

'Icelandic'

The idea was to create a look that would relate to music, the different countries participating and Iceland. The designers researched the basic forms of Höfðaletur, a unique Icelandic font of wood-carved capital letters dating back to the 16th century, and used its base to design their own type, Rich Hard. This type was then used to make the whole design concept of the music festival. Like Höfðaletur, the designers used Rich Hard as a decorative font and write Icelandic names of the instruments, by that relating to music as well as to raise foreign guests' interest to visit the country for the festival.

On the poster as well as the cover you can read the Icelandic names of the instruments, from the top left downwards. This also made the design 'fun' in a way since there could be hidden words in Icelandic. It is not easy to read like Höfðaletur was, unless you give yourself some time to look at it.

T: Nordic Music Days
   Iceland
D: Siggi Orri
   Thorhannesson
C: Nordic Music Days
W: Promotion
L: English, Icelandic
Y: 2006

'Identity'

3 different projects for
the contemporary art
gallery Loevenbruck,
Paris. The designer
usually works on their
invitation cards for
collective exhibitions,
or when the idea is
not to reproduce the
artists' visuals on
the card. It is more a
typographic project,
without photos, to
create an identity for
the exhibition itself.

T:1.5 ans seulement déjà
  2.Big
  3.Bruno Peinado. Me,
  buysellf & I
D:Sylvia Tournerie
C:Loevenbruck gallery,
  Paris
W:Preview cards
Y:2006

1

2

3

'Illusion'

This 'drama' poster
parallels death, love
and sleep. The little
set is built around a
store bough picture
frame and uses paper to
construct the physical
lettering.

T:Illusion Type
D:FromKtoJ/FromJtoK
C:FromKtoJ/FromJtoK
W:Poster
L:English
Y:2006

'Implements'

This display typeface
is designed with glass
installation in mind.
Ideally the 2 colours
could be applied to
different panes of
glass. By place the
pains no more than one
foot apart the blue
and beige patterns
allow 2 levels to read.
From one perspective
the typeface serves
as ornamentation. From
another perspective,
by aligning the blue
and beige patterns,
legible messaging is
revealed.

T: Implements of
   Wonder Type
D: FromKtoJ/FromJtoK
C: FromKtoJ/FromJtoK
W: Display typeface
L: English
Y: 2007

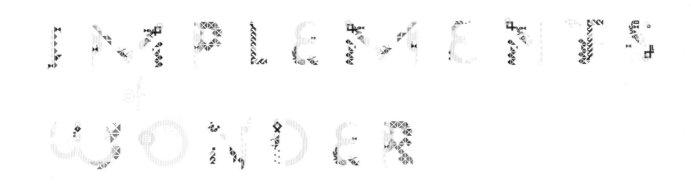

'Installation'

USCA is the one of the biggest moments for the Commercial Radio every year. In order to show the alphabets 'ABCD' in the promotion slogan are competition grades for the award as well as voting choices, designers decided to make props and then photo-shoot them as the main visuals. They spent a huge portion of the budget on this. Unfortunately, they found that the promotion of the MTV Music Awards was using the exactly same approach as they do right after the satisfactory props were produced. But since the designers understand that this kind of situation happens occasionally, they decided to keep their original ideas at the end.

T:USCA (Ultimate
  Song Chart Awards)
  Presentation 2006
D:Artroom - Commercial
  Radio Productions Ltd.
C:Manhattan Id
W:Installation, Poster
L:Chinese, English
Y:2006

M A N H A T T A N **id** 信用咭

06年度
叱咤樂壇流行榜
頒獎典禮
Ultimate Song Chart Awards Presentation 2006
ABCD一點即光 樂壇亮燈由你主持

06年度
叱咤樂壇流行榜
頒獎典禮
Ultimate Song Chart Awards Presentation 2006
ABCD一點即光 樂壇亮燈由你主持

'Interiors'

'Interiors' was originally conceived as a digital font and was inspired by an old wooden chair in the corner of Byrom's office that, when looked at it from a certain angle, resembled the letter 'h.' Using the 3-dimensional principles and closely adhering to type design conventions, 26 letters of the alphabet were drawn and generated. Later the characters were constructed in three dimensions using tubular steel into full-scale furniture frames. The end result becomes almost freestyle furniture design.

———————————————

T: Interiors
D: Andrew Byrom
C: Andrew Byrom
W: 3D typeface
L: English
Y: 2003

'Invention'

The typeface that stemmed
from the designer
original poster 'Meaning
is Made.' Geometry has
always fascinated the
designer, in school it
was the only math subject
he could make sense
from, it seems natural
to make a typeface using
the simplest geometric
shapes.

T:Re-Invent the Alphabet
D:Widmest
C:Widmest
W:Print
L:English
Y:2007

Re-invent the alphabet.

'Isometric'

The idea was to make a wallpaper/pattern that would completely change the studio at school. A font was created in 3 isometric views and then glued up one letter at the time to cover all the walls. The letters were put up randomly, but in-between you will find some of the 20-30 words spelled out, like Debbie Does Dallas, Kaffi and all of the designers' names.

———————————————————

T: Wallpaper
D: Iceland Academy of
   the Arts, graphic
   design graduation
   class of 2006
C: Iceland Academy
   of the Arts
W: Typography, Pattern
   design
L: English, Icelandic
Y: 2006

J

'Japanese'

1.The book is made
for celebrating the
10th anniversary of
the motion graphic
studio called WOW Inc.
Digital video works of
WOW from the past 10
years are translated
and assembled in a
2-dimensional and
printable form; a
DVD is included too.
5 artists who WOW
respects: Shigeki
Hattori (Graf),
Yoshio Kubo, Gwenael
Nicolas(Curiosity),
Masafumi Ishiwata,
Koichiro
Tanaka(projector) and
Artless joined and
developed the theme
'Next 10 years' for
this book.

2.Graphics collaged
with Japanese plants
and trees are placed
on numbers. The
designer used numbers
as a flower vase and
expressed four seasons
from 0 to 10. For
that, even numbers
are collaged with
photography and uneven
numbers are collaged
with illustration.

T:1.WOW10
　2.WOW10 numbers
D:artless Inc.
C:WOW Inc.
W:1.Art book
　2.Typography, Collage
L:1.English, Japanese
　2.Japanese
Y:2007

'Kerning'

The studio was
approached by the
International Society
of Typographic
Designers to create
a piece of work to
be exhibited in an
exhibition entitled
'My City, My London'
which was part of
The London Design
Festival 2006. The
exhibition celebrated
the place of graphic
design in contemporary
visual culture and
its intention was to
explore typography in
the visual world of
the capital.

The designers'
solution was simple
– a typographic map of
London.

T:London's Kerning
D:NB: Studio
C:International Society
  of Typographic
  Designers
W:Poster
L:English
Y:2006

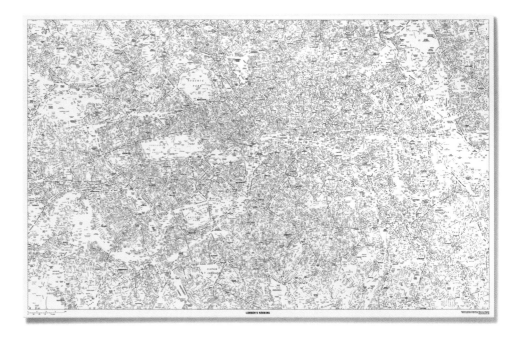

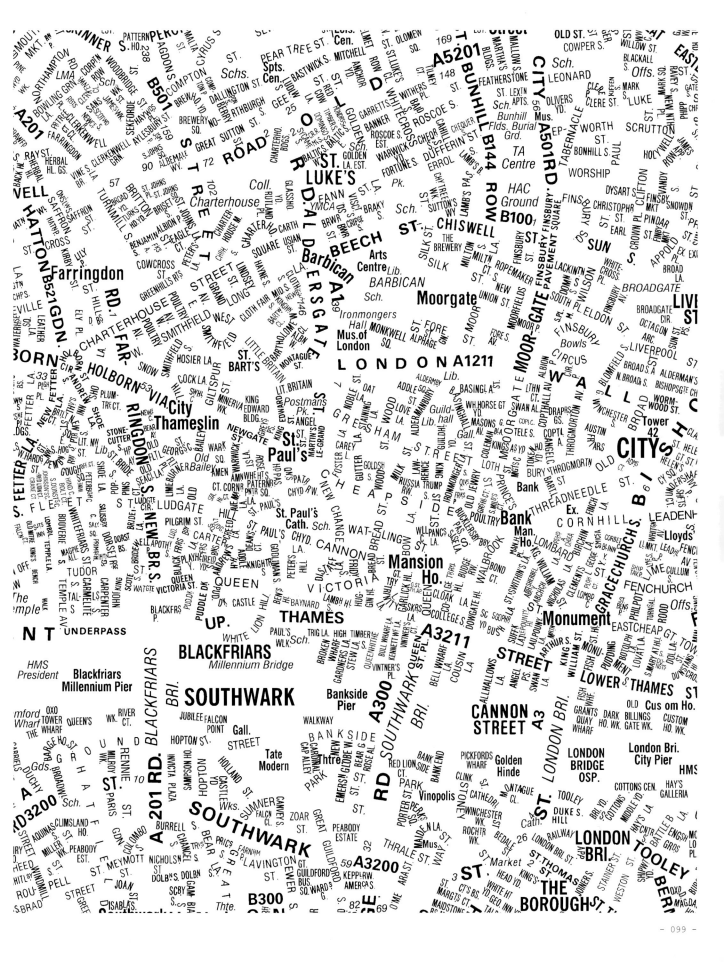

'Lace'

The Wish display
face is inspired by
contemporary lace.
The custom font is
engineered to hold all
intricate details when
laser cut.

T:Wish Type
D:FromKtoJ/FromJtoK
C:FromKtoJ/FromJtoK
W:Display typeface
L:English
Y:2006

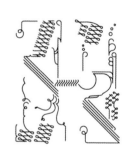

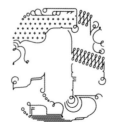

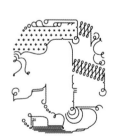

'Lantern'

Osaka Design Pack aimed at inviting young Asian designers to design specific posters for a local cultural event. The designer were asked to design for the 'Bon' festival, a traditional Japanese summer dance festival. The idea is to create a 'poster lantern' with the Japanese typography – 'bon' inspired from the Japanese 'Yakuta' belt. When posters are hanged together, it would appear as real lanterns with people dancing along the street.

T: Osaka Design Pack
  – 'Big Bon!'
D: Milkxhake
C: Osaka Design Pack,
  Japan
W: Poster
L: Japanese
Y: 2006

'Lecturing'

Poster promoting a
design lecture given
by Post Typography at
Susquehanna University.
Being the middle of
winter in the mountains
of Pennsylvania,
the designers grew
impressive beards to
help stave off the
cold.

T: Beards Rule
D: Post Typography
C: Susquehanna University
W: Poster
L: English
Y: 2005

'Life'

It can transform from
the Kanji character to
the English character,
or the other way round
with the same meaning
but without excess and
deficiencies of parts.

———————————————

T:Life
D:Dainippon Type
  Organization
C:Dainippon Type
  Organization
W:3D typeface
L:Englisn, Japanese
Y:2006

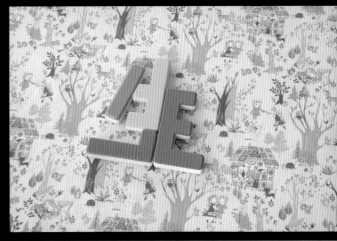

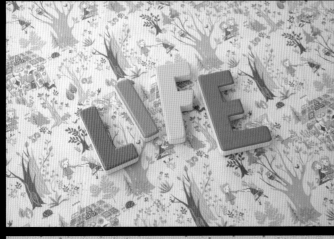

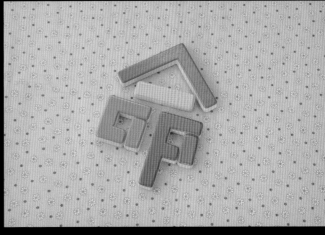

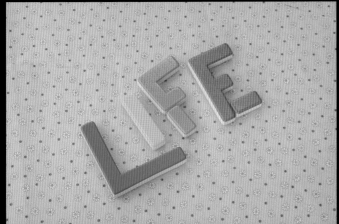

'Light'

NBLight™ is a computer programmed typeface which was derived from a light installation by Dutch designer Jarrik Muller and Stefan Gandl.

Diverse neon bulbs are used to form a simple matrix which is used to create the entire alphabet. NBLight™ contains 255 characters (upper case only).

T: NBLight™
D: Neubau
   (NeubauBerlin.Com)
C: NeubauLaden.com
W: Illustration
Y: 2006

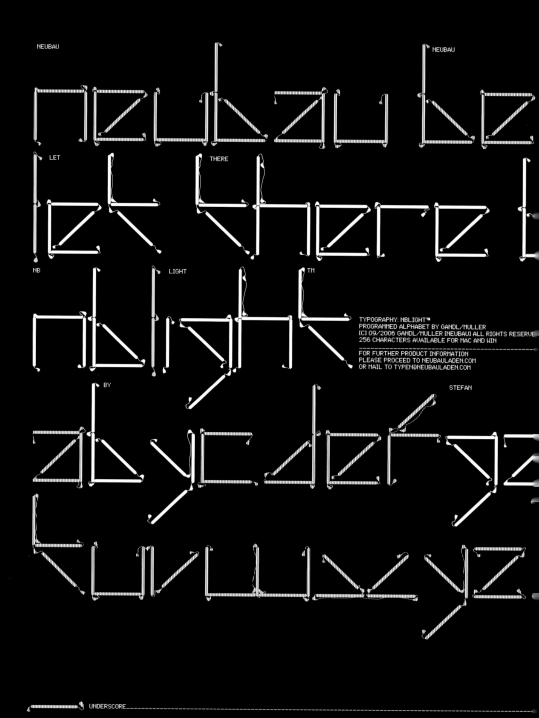

JARRIK

adt nullers
0123456789 0-9

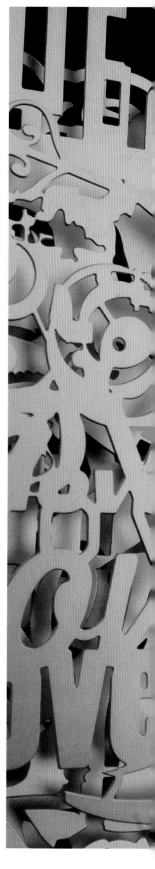

'Love'

The word 'love' is written in all the possible ways to express the idea of 'I love you' as the designer believes that true love never dies. The first prototype of this brooch was made in 2003. It has been revisited, improved and made wearable.

T: Love Heart
D: Tjep.
C: Tjep.
W: 3D brooch design
L: English
M: 12x12x1cm

'Media'

Microwave is a new media-arts organization based in Hong Kong showcases classical and cutting-edge new media-arts from around the world. The designers created a totally new identity and designed all promotional items for the Festival in 2006 based on a new custom-made typography with fluorescent orange and green. The new image emphasizes a dynamic identity with vision and sustainability.

T:Microwave
  International New
  Media Arts Festival
  2006
D:Milkxhake
C:Microwave
W:Event identity
L:English, Chinese
Y:2006

live!

microwave live!
fever soul   13.11 (mon)

time: 2100 · late
venue: 10 St. Francis
address: 10 St. Francis Street, Wanchai
$40 at door

audio: Techno/Electric (soft + hard) to jam
visual: Procedural Animation Projection

performers:
· Teoh + VJ aplha
· theDemos + SIG
· Special guest

www.microwavefest.net

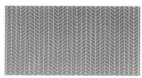

ANIMATRONICA
漫話引力

microwave
international
new
media arts
festival
微波國際新媒體藝術節

4-15 nov 2006
hong kong

'Medieval'

The annual 'Random Cube' club profile was made strictly typographical. The typeface Midi Evil was created for this purpose, loosely based on medieval letters. The live music was a great mix of drones, noise rock impro to folk electronic music. A clash of everything, just like the typeface. Printed in gold and reflex blue.

T: Random Cube 2006
D: Grandpeople
C: Random Cube Festival
W: Visual profile
Y: 2006

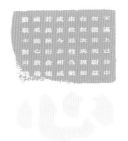

慈悲
Mercy

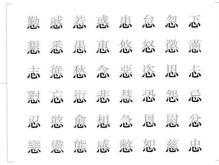

'Mercy'

The design illustrates the idea that oneself could take up any challenges in life and face to different emotional feelings with a mercy attitude.

T: Untitled
D: CoDesign Ltd
C: Peace of Mind Mercy Foundation
W: Logotype, Stationery
L: Chinese
Y: 2005

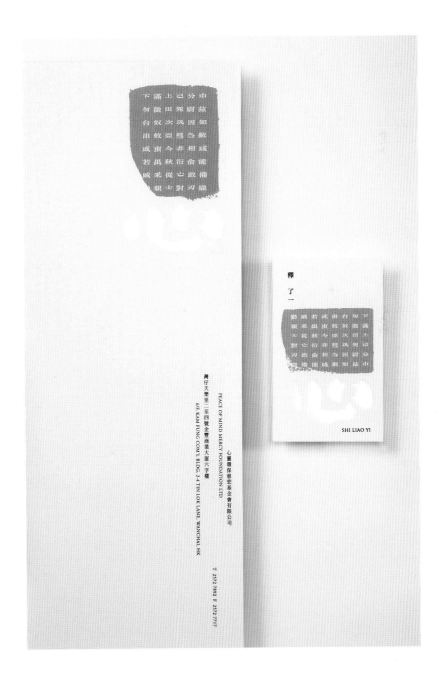

'Milky'

Image for the 'Talent
Channel 4 Book,' which
represents 'The 11
'Clock Show,' a famous
Channel 4 comedy pro-
gram. The client wanted
to represent the name
of the comedians who
work in the program.
The designers created a
milky, cheesy and funny
scene, where there is
a bomb at 11:00 in a
milky surface.

T:Milky Comedy Splash
D:Serial Cut™
C:Channel 4 UK
W:3D typeface
L:English
Y:2007

'Mince'

Alphabets completed
while enrolled in
the Communications
Design Department
at Pratt Institute.
Each character was
shaped, wrapped,
and photographed
individually.

T:Value Pack
D:Robert J. Bolesta
C:Robert J. Bolesta
W:Typeface
Y:2005

1

'Misprint'

1.Splash page for
misprintedtype.com

2.Artwork created for
an art show.

3.A personal work of
the designer.

T:1.MisprintedType
   2.Everything Will Be
   Just Fine
   3.Greed
D:Misprinted Type
C:Misprinted Type
W:1,2.Drawing
   3.Drawing, Collage
L:English
Y:1.2002
   2.2006
   3.2007

2

'Miss'

A book with the collected work of performance artist Catti Brandelius alter ego Miss Universum.

T: Miss Universum
D: Hjärta Smärta
C: Ordfront Publishing
  House
W: Book
L: Swedish
Y: 2005

'Mug'

Build was initially
commissioned to produce
the identity for a
new online shop called
'TYPE' which based in
Hong Kong. The idea of
the shop was to sell
beautifully made prod-
ucts with a typographic
leaning by differ-
ent designers. After
completing the brand-
ing, Build was asked
to design the launch
range of products for
the store based on its
range, boldly around
different typefaces.

T:TYPE products
D:Build
C:TYPE, Hong Kong
W:Branding, Product
  design
L:English
Y:2006

'Music'

This is a contemporary music concert organized by a French musician, who is now living and teaching in Tokyo. As the theme of the concert is about poems written by a Greek poet, Sappho, and a Greek composer, Xenakis, the designer made use of the poems with Greek alphabets and also some Japanese translation of the poems as the main elements of the design. He made changes to the size of the text and placed them on the harpsichord and the stage floor to make the design looked like coming out from the harpsichord and flowing around the space. At the same time, the design was made to combine with other objects in the space and became the shadow of the objects and other musical instruments.

T:Clavecin+Percussion
  III
D:Tsang Kin-wah
C:Tsang Kin-wah
W:Stage design
Y:2006

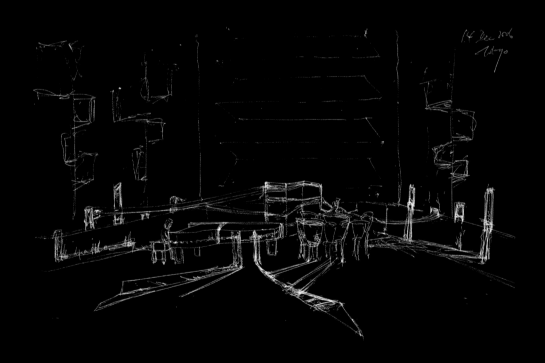

'Neon'

'Interiors Light' was inspired by Marcel Breuer's 'Wassily Chair' and was originally to be constructed from rounded chrome tubular steel. As Byrom progressed he realized that by thinking on a smaller scale it could be constructed in neon. The limitations of working in neon is tough on the original design so he needed to rework the design several times, embracing the constraints of this beautiful and delicate material.

T: Interiors Light
D: Andrew Byrom
C: Andrew Byrom
W: 3D typeface
L: English
Y: 2005

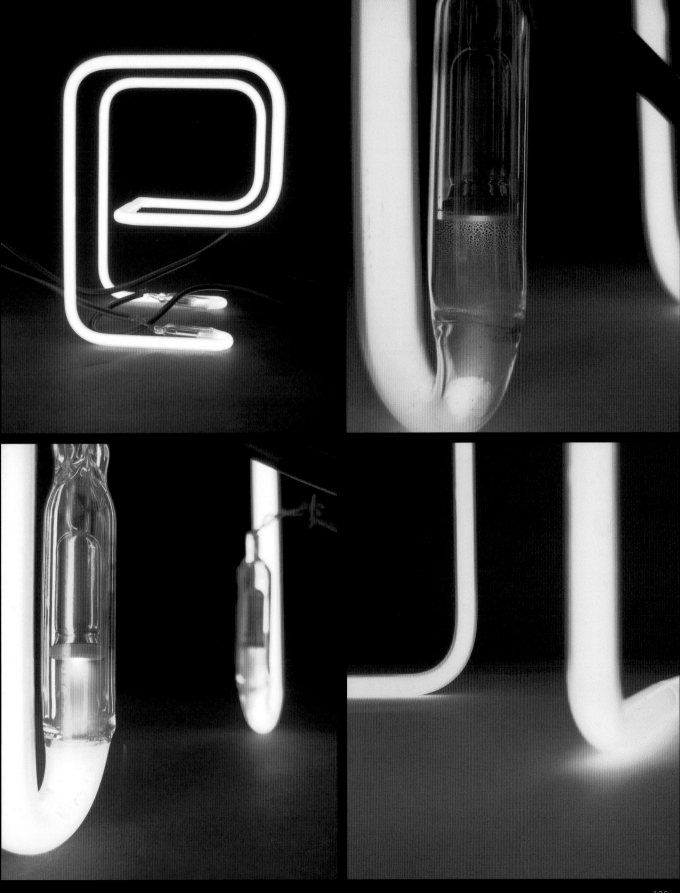

abcde
fghijk
lmnop
qrstuv
wxyz

'New'

Phonetic play for
Command+N charrette. A
group of collaborating
designers were asked to
contribute work around
the theme 'new.'

T:NEW!
D:Apirat Infahsaeng
C:Command+N
W:Poster
L:English
Y:2007

WE BARELY
KNEW
THEE

'Night'

Guy designed a series of posters inviting designers to a fiction-al event - Designer's Night in Tel Aviv. The invitational posters are built from photo-graphs of fluorescent and home lights rear-ranged into letters. The designer loves the fact that when you look closely at the posters you can see things like home floor and power plugs.

───────────────

T: Designer's Night in
   Tel Aviv
D: Guy Haviv
C: Guy Haviv
W: Poster
L: Hebrew
Y: 2007

לילה לבן למעצבים
סדנאות | הרצאות | השראה

19.07.07, בין חמישי לשישי
מחצות עד הזריחה
רחבת מוזיאון תל־אביב

תחרות כרזות לילית
במסגרת לילה לבן למעצבים

19.07.07, בין חמישי לשישי
מחצות עד הזריחה
רחבת מוזיאון תל־אביב

icograda

תחרות כרזות לילית
במסגרת לילה לבן למעצבים

19.07.07, בין חמישי לשישי
מחצות עד הזריחה
רחבת מוזיאון תל־אביב

icograda ראד ⧉ ⛨

'Nordic'

Combining the simplest
elements with organic
forms to produce a new
Chinese typeface to
echo with Scandinavian
design.

T:Nordic Alive Typeface
D:Hamlet Au-Yeung
C:Hamlet Au-Yeung
W:Typeface
L:Chinese
Y:2005

私 今 日 考 新 案 發

明 品 一 語 四 十 五

抱 燈 文 書 內 限 定

本 導 了 恃 學 友 愛

母 兄 妹 大 間 我 國

小 賢 句 口 永 記 他

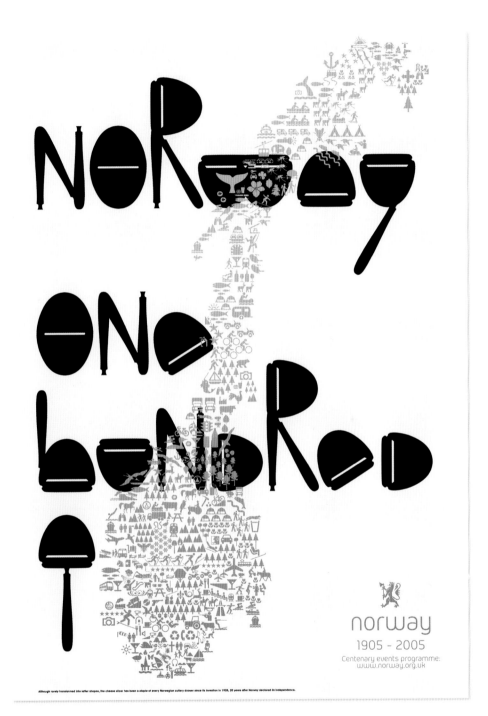

'Norway'

The poster is made to celebrate the Norway's centenary. It is printed with black and gold ink.

T: Norway 100
D: Non-Format
C: The Royal Norwegian
   Embassy, London
W: Poster
L: English
Y: 2006

'Number'

Poster design for the
brand 'Fayte.'

T: Life and Number.
   Number and Life
D: Sixstation
C: Fayte
W: Poster
L: Chinese
Y: 2007

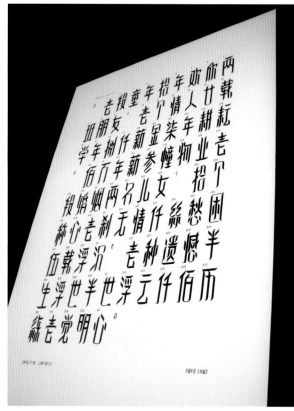

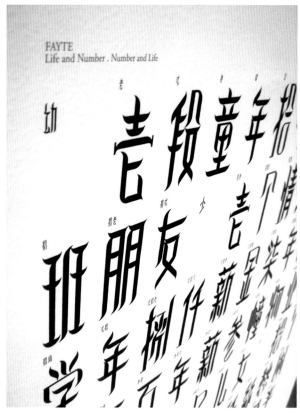

幼 壹 段 童 年 捨 年 欢 你 两

班 朋 友 少 壹 个 情 人 廿 载

学 年 捌 仟 薪 昱 柒 年 耕 耘

青 佰 万 年 薪 参 幢 物 业 壹

段 婚 姻 两 名 儿 女 中 捨 个

补 心 壹 刹 无 情 仟 丝 愁 困

伍 载 浮 沉 老 壹 种 遗 憾 半

生 浮 世 半 世 浮 云 仟 佰 历

练 壹 觉 明 心 终

仟种可能 万事可能　人生如字 字中人生

'Objects'

Making a poster with
any kinds of objects
in 2 hours.

T:AinsiFont
D:Atelier télescopique
C:AinsiFont. Digitale
  Type Foundry
W:Poster
L:English, French
Y:2007

'On'

Fifty ceiling lights
form an illuminated
'ON.' A lighting
installation designed
as the key visual for
the launch of the
desres design group.
It is used on posters,
flyers and the start
screen of the website.

T: desres is on
D: desres design group
C: desres design group
W: Installation
L: English
Y: 2006

'October'

PDF Calendar design for design portal and ezine 'Lounge72.' The designer was invited to create one of the 12 months – October.

T: 玖別 (September is gone)
D: Sixstation
C: Lounge72
W: Poster
L: Chinese
Y: 2005

'Online'

Online logo created for
Accept & Proceed design
studio as part of the
Accept & Proceed logo
ongoing project.

T:Accept & Proceed
D:Si Scott Design
C:Accept & Proceed
W:Online logo
L:English
Y:2006

'Organic'

The concept for this typeface was to create seemingly organic forms using digital technology. Using only a scanner, some tape and most importantly a notecard each letter was created. Using the tape, a grid was marked out on the scanner glass. As the scanner belt moved, the designer moved the notecard folding it, bending it and rolling it but always sticking to the grid. The images were then bitmapped so they could be applied to fontographer and be used. It is not a practical typeface and only exists as an upper case, however, the project was more about the process than the final result.

_____

T:Scan Note
D:David Lane
C:David Lane
W:Typeface
L:English
Y:2006

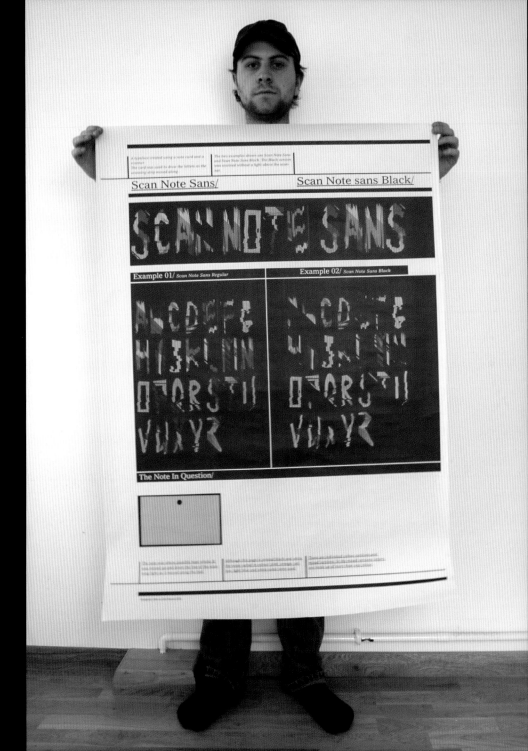

'Out'

This is a poster taken from a current series of personal works which are produced in very small numbers and given as gifts to friends.

T: You Make the Sun
   Come Out
D: Adam Hayes
C: Adam Hayes
W: Hand-lettered poster
L: English
Y: 2007

'Party'

A series of 3 flyers
designed to promote the
designer's birthday
party. Sort of a funny
realization of the
concept 'life before
and after August
17.' Combining retro
found images together
with doodle sort of
typography.

T:AUG 17 party flyers
D:Corp.Unit
C:Corp.Unit
W:Flyer
L:English
Y:2002

of poster exhibition
project initiated by
Art4Soul from Malaysia.
The poster is based on
the same theme for the
exhibition.'Pray&Pay'
illustrates the
relationship between
religion superstition
and Chinese people.
The design is purely
inspired from the
traditional paper money
for ancestor 'Yuen
Bo.' People 'pay' as
in 'pray' to God.

T:Pray&Pay
D:Milkxhake
C:Art4Soul, Malaysia
W:Poster
L:English
Y:2006

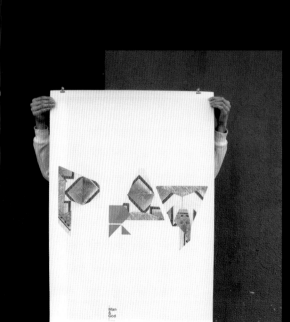

'Peace'

Poster approached
peace and environment
by original alphabet
composed by dots.

———————————

T: Peace
D: Taste Inc.
C: Taste Inc.
W: Poster
L: English
Y: 2003

Though the 21st century has begun, the situation which mankind's war and terrorism, the destruction of the environment, the atomic energy pollution and the mass murder don't end in is an important problem. Mankind's consciousness decides the future destiny of the earth. As for understanding a difference in the religion, it is the first step to wipe away racial discrimination. It is the important point for mankind to coexist in this earth environment. It becomes the start of mankind's new history.

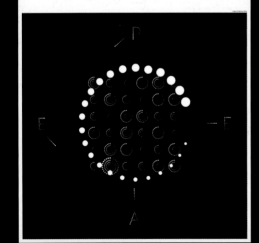

'Performance'

Poster announcing
Piebald's performance.

T:Piebald
D:Apirat Infahsaeng
C:Manic Productions
  for Piebald
W:Poster
L:English
Y:2007

'Plastic'

This font was made
for a plastic surgery
clinic. Each letter is
an illustration of a
word, for example B for
Botox, S for Silicone
or N for Nip/Tuck.

T:Beautiful
D:Florence Tétier (Whaa)
C:Ecal (University of
  Arts of Lausanne)
W:Typeface
L:English
Y:2007

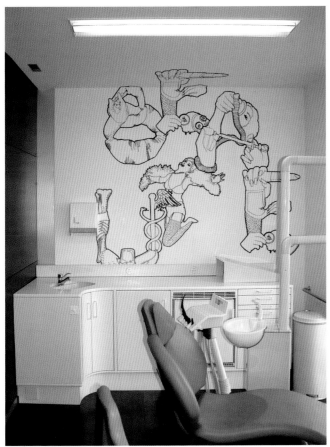

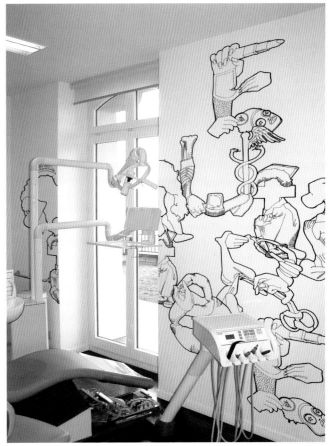

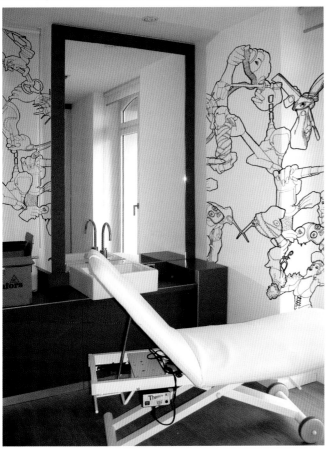

'Plyke'

A series of posters
created by hand and
then printed on
black plyke board in
phosphorescent ink.

T: 100% Design Tokyo
   Exhibition
D: Si Scott Design
C: 100% design week
   Tokyo/designers block
W: Exhibition
L: English
Y: 2006

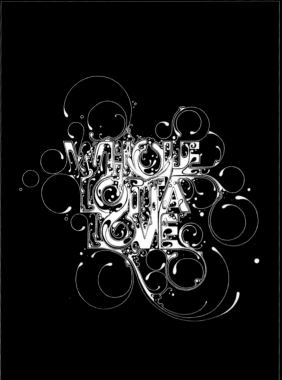

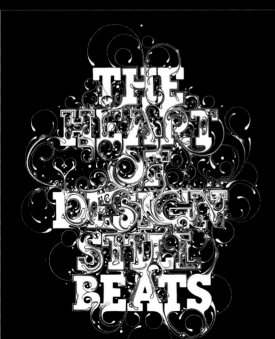

'Poem'

Experimental typography
work mixed with Chinese
poem in modern typography.

_____

T: 滿江紅 (Manjianghong)
D: Sixstation
C: Sixstation
W: Poster
L: Chinese
Y: 2007

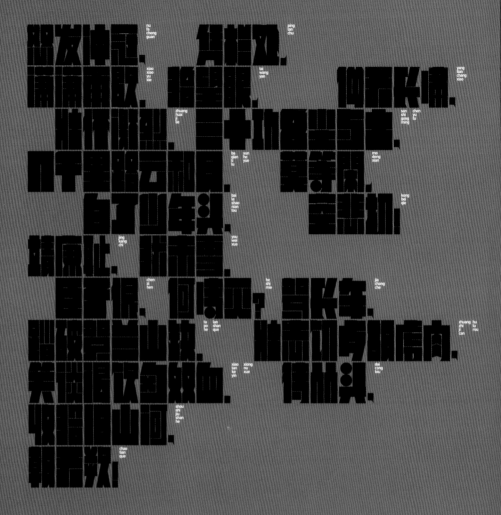

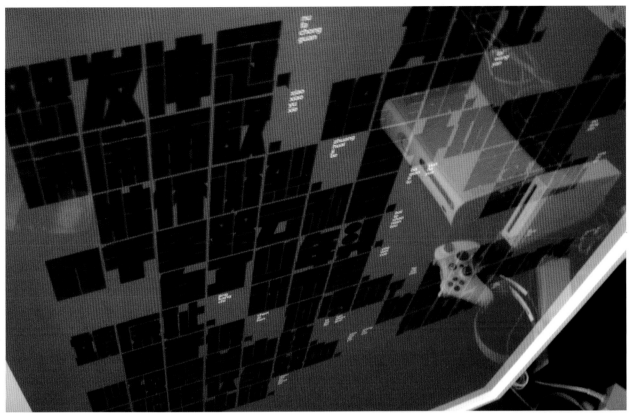

'Poet'

Poster exhibition by
24 designers who make
poetry by poet motif.
Posters in B0 size were
put in the underground
of a shopping center
and the extension
of it formed into
environmental design.

T:Dog's name often
  'Character designer
  of/Kanayo Ueda and 24
  poets'
D:Taste Inc.
C:Kanayo Ueda
W:Poster
L:Japanese
Y:2004

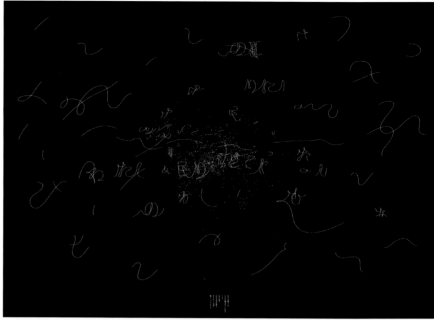

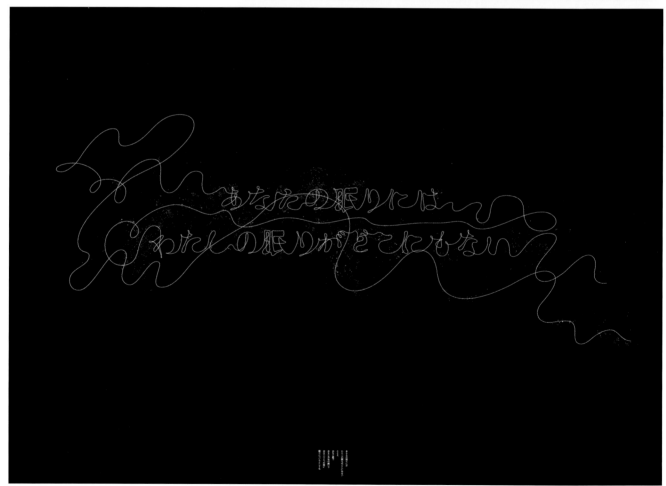

'Pompei'

Poster and catalogue
for the 37th
International Theatre
Festival.

T: Pompei
D: Non-Format
C: VENICE BIENNALE
W: Poster, Catalogue
L: English, Italian
Y: 2005

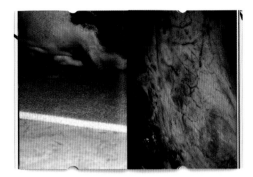

'Pop-up'

Byrom TSS is a 'pop-up' temporary signage system. Each letter is fabricated from waterproof nylon wrapped around a fiberglass pole frame (similar to the construction of a modern dome tent). An elastic cord running inside the hollow poles allows the design to collapse into a small bag for storage. The design is intended for use in shops, galleries, festivals, conferences etc.

T: Byrom TSS
D: Andrew Byrom
C: Andrew Byrom
W: Temporary signage
   system, 3D typeface
L: English
Y: 2007

ABCDEFGHIJ
KLMNOPQRST
UVWXYZ

'Prize'

D&AD commissioned the designers to devise a new campaign for promoting and boosting membership over their 5 different categories. The challenge was to devise a concept that would appeal to the design community, from art directors to students. The concept had to have a distinct look and feel that would translate well over various forms of print, as well as online. The message had to be clear and concise, as some of the target audience may not have heard of D&AD and its membership. The designers' solution was to highlight the benefits of being a member by literally showing people what they could get for their money. The concept loosely based on a parody of popular family game shows, referencing the stack of prizes (but minus the beautiful assistant). The designers wanted people to be reminded of the D&AD membership, so they decided to have the leaflets double up as posters that people could display, as opposed to just receiving a leaflet which would inevitably be tucked away in a corner.

T: D&AD Membership
   Campaign
D: NB: Studio
C: D&AD
W: Poster, Postcard,
   Online
Y: 2006

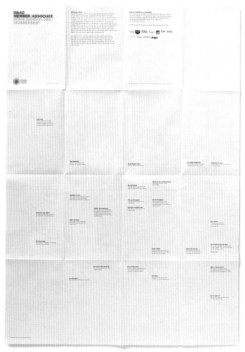

'Punch'

Because 'classic' and 'antis' are not sold in pairs, the wholesale buying process will result in waste. The 'Waste Collation' system is employed to re-design garments a subsequent collection beginning with the waste garment components. Material By Product believes in intelligent design, not fashion whimsy. The essence of its design sensibilities is steeped within the traditions of bespoke tailoring and the essential realities and reconsidered design potentials of a 'piece of cloth.' 3 Deep Design was asked to document the collection and create an original typeface that would reflect the intensely crafted approach of the company and the collection.

T:Material By Product,
  Punch Out
D:3 Deep Design
C:Material By Product
W:Publication
Y:2006

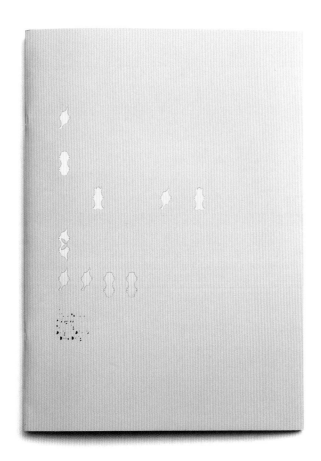

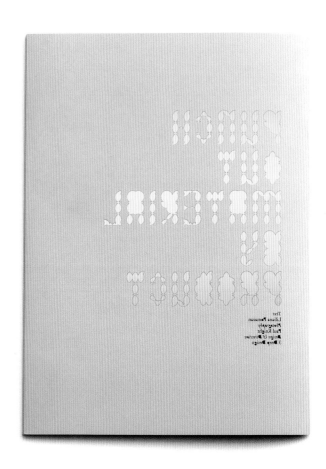

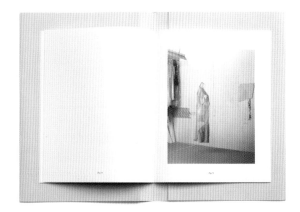

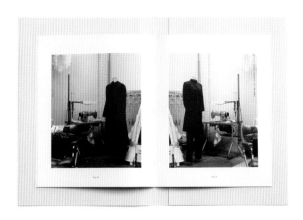

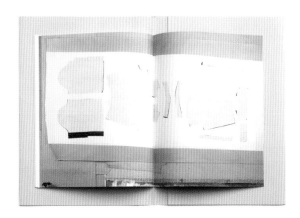

'Puti'

This work is a typographic interpretation of 2 poems quoted from the original Zen classic, The Platform Sutra of the 6th Patriarch, that dates back almost 1500 years ago. This is a Chinese philosophy-from Buddism. The general idea is to believe everything is the same in the world and nothing really has a shape or appearance, so where could dust come from if there is actually purely nothing in the world?

T:The Puti Tree
D:Khaki Creative &
  Design, Inc.
C:Khaki Creative &
  Design, Inc.
W:Typeface
L:Chinese
Y:2006

菩提
本無樹

"Actually, the Puti tree does not exist..."

亦非 明鏡
臺

"... nor does anything exist in the mirror."

本來
無一
物

"Here, now, nothing exists..."

何處
惹塵
埃

"... so how might there be dust?"

'Quarter'

Poster Magazine was a quarterly magazine at the vanguard of Australian fashion, art, architecture and design. Having evolved dramatically since its inception in 2001, Poster Magazine was a printed forum for the discussion, presentation and critique of Australian culture. 3 Deep Design demonstrated the sheer diversity of the editorial approach and the ethos and energy behind the design of the magazine. 3 Deep Design no longer art directs this magazine.

T:Poster Magazine
D:3 Deep Design
C:Poster Magazine
W:Editorial
Y:2006

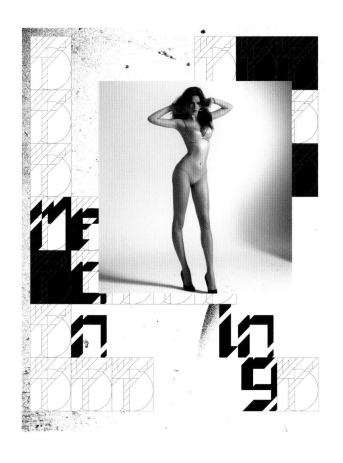

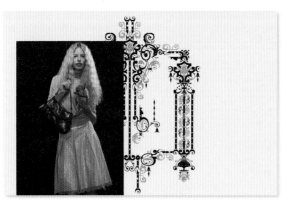

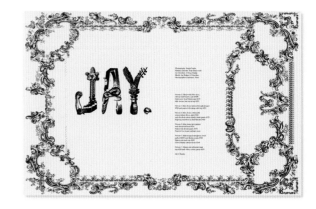

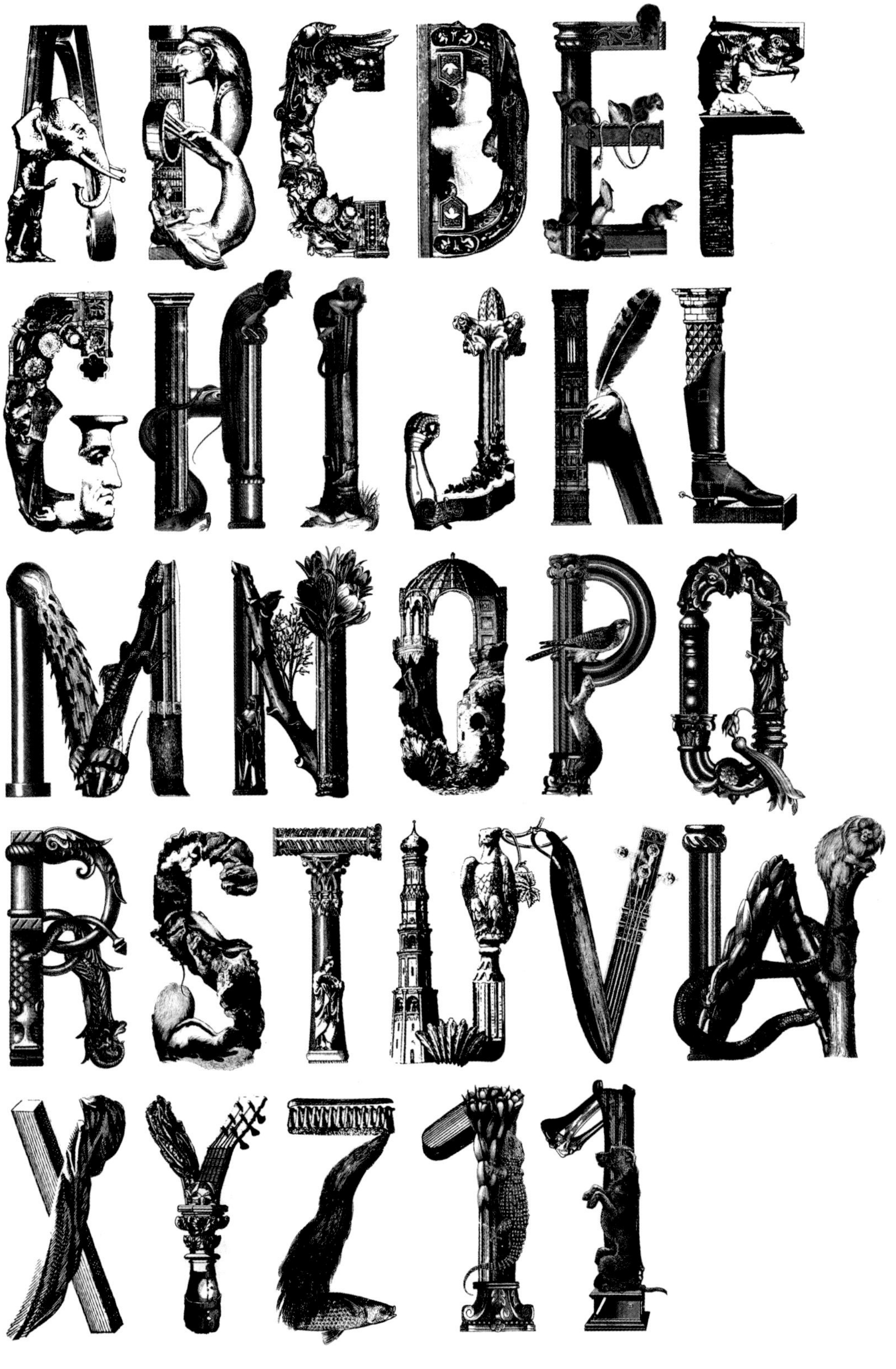

'Radio'

Artroom always try
their best not to only
use the existing types
in their designs if
time is sufficient,
the designers
believe astonishing
typographic approach
can make design shines
on stage. Here the
designers randomly
picked different
typographic designs
throughout the years
among the plentiful
inspiring projects.

T:Chinese logotypes
D:Artroom - Commercial
  Radio Productions Ltd.
C:Commercial Radio
  Productions Ltd.
W:Logotype
L:Chinese, English
Y:2002-7

'Real'

To promote Beeffeater's drink in every WET issue, the designer is asked to develop an idea based on a particular theme. For the 1st issue, Serial Cut™ was given a theme about 'Night' to work with. All photographed elements were real, so the final result was a photographic collage, with elements that had been scanned, printed and cut (falcon, deer), and Helvetica typography made from plastic and real elements (pink strips, straws, ice cubes, glasses, diskette...). This collage could have easily been done with Photoshop, but was actually done in a photography studio, and was barely retouched digitally. It is something like 'photographed graphic design,' in a sophisticated blue and magenta atmosphere. A 20-page promo magazine is produced for the first non-dry gin in the world: WET by Beefeater.

The publication was created by DressLab, designed by Albert Folch, and distributed in the coolest fashion stores and clubs.

T: WET
D: Serial Cut™
C: Beeffeater
W: Promo Magazine
L: English
Y: 2006

NIGHT COMES TO ME

I CAME FROM NIGHT

WET QUEST LIST

WEAR IT AT NIGHT
DOWNLOAD IT AT SERIALCUT.COM/WET

'Revolutionize'

Announcing Brian Collins' travelling lecture 'Design Changes Everything' at various design schools around the nation. The piece is a visualization and documentation of the process of creation, exploration, struggle, self-doubt, and the final crystallization of inspiration into form.

T: Design Changes
   Everything,
   Everywhere, Always,
   Sometimes, Never
D: Apirat Infahsaeng
C: Brian Collins,
   Executive Creative
   Director, BIG
W: Poster
L: English
Y: 2007

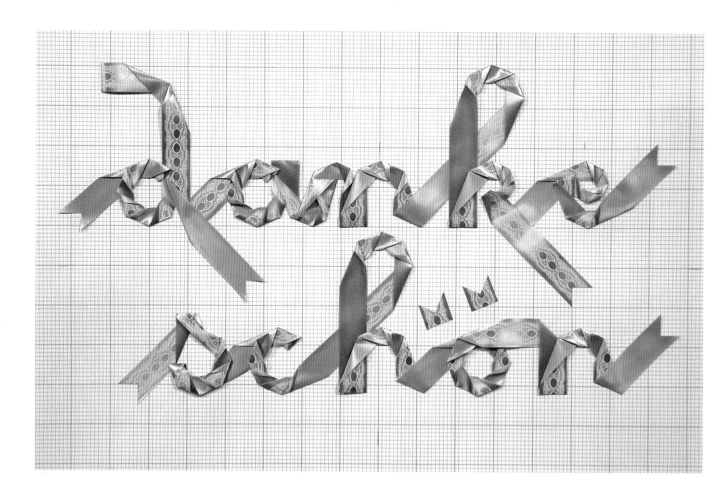

'Ribbon'

Paulette is a script ribbon typeface with corresponding folding templates.

T: Paulette (folded)
D: FromKtoJ/FromJtoK
C: FromKtoJ/FromJtoK
W: Typeface, Folding templates, Poster
L: English
Y: 2006

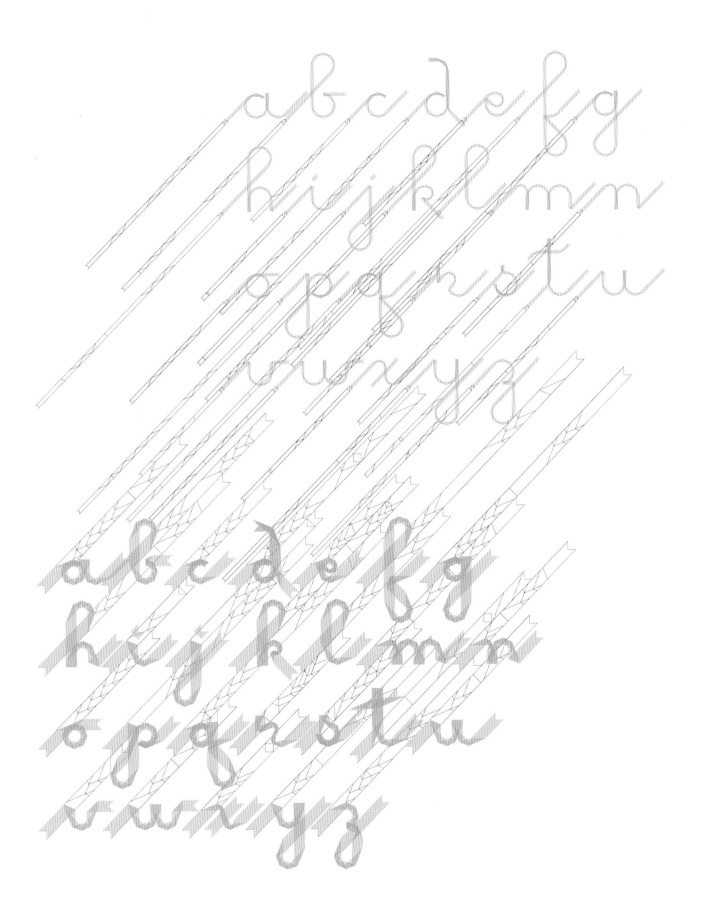

'Scotch'

The designer created
the logo of Tropic
Blues Band, printed in
a natural size (6x2.5m)
on 120 A4 sheets. They
recalled the logo on
floor, envisaged and
redrawn the whole with
Scotch Tape.

The band came one day
and let the designers
roll them up with Scotch
Tape. The music of TETBB
is a mixture of psycho-
billy-punky-blues,
completely anchored
in the Seventies. The
designers found out that
they like Whisky, so
they used Scotch.

T:The Experimental
  Tropic Blues Band/
  Dynamite Boogie
D:pleaseletmedesign
C:The Experimental
  Tropic Blues Band
W:1.Album cover,
  2.Inside booklet,
  Poster
L:English
Y:2006

1

The Experimental
Tropic Blues Band

1. Rena The Renegade
2. Jealous Rock
3. Rising From The Dead
4. The Gambler
5. Twice Blues
6. Voodoo Rise
7. Gangrene Blues
8. Garbage Man
9. Snake Pit
10. Dry Country
11. Heartbreak
12. Mojito Green Blues
13. I Went Down
14. Evil Don't Go Home

'Sculpture'

1. A 3-dimensional word, 'WAR' made of ash tree branches, commercial wood, paint and blue bullets for building (red, white and blue). This piece is the 4th in a series, one each year since March 2003, in protest of the American war in Iraq.

2. A 3-dimensional word, 'ART' made of various fruit woods doweled. Collected by Charles Breyer in San Francisco, California, it is created for a Judge in the US Federal District Court in San Francisco, California.

3. A 3-dimensional symbol for the word, 'AND' made of apple prunings from a fruit grower in Northern California. It is painted with inks and constructed with screws.

4. A 3-dimensional letter of the alphabet made of manzanita branches and bullets for building (screws).

5. A 3-dimensional ampersand symbol made of apple tree pruning, paint and copper roofing nails.

6. An ampersand, a 3-dimensional symbol for the word, 'AND' made of ash branches and screws.

T: 1. Globalization IV: Collateral Damage
   2. Art Rules
   3. Estuary
   4. Big Question
   5. Past Tense
   6. GO and ...
D: Gyöngy Laky
C: Gyöngy Laky
W: Sculpture
L: English
M: 1. 32x97x4inches
   2. 8x14x4.5inches
   3. 35x34x3.5inches
   4. 68x78x5inches
   5. 22.5x22.5x3inches
   6. 40x46x4inches
Y: 1. 2006
   2. 2001
   3,4,6. 2007
   5. 2004

1

2

3

4

5

6

'Signage'

Visual identity and
signage system of the
New Highschool Guy
Debeyre building.

T: Guy Debeyre Highschool
D: Atelier télescopique
C: Communauté Urbaine de
   Dunkerque, Luc
   Delemazure Architectes
W: Graphic language
L: French
Y: 2006-7

'Shaolin'

T-shirt design series
for GMTEE. The theme
is about 60's HK film's
fighting scene.

_____

T:Shaolin
D:Sixstation
C:Atomicsushi
W:T-shirt graphic
Y:2005

'Silence'

The starting point is the installation series 'Sounds of Silence' that turns various forms of silence into a sensory experience. The documentation of this project should provide an original interpretation of the subject that transcends the descriptive approach.

This book extends the concept of the installation series in a formal sense. The 4 installations of the series, each of them autonomous, are represented by 4 associative booklets – accompanied by texts of various authors, photographs of the project and a cinematic documentation on DVD. A multiply wrapped cover combines these diverse aspects into a comprehensive book whose diversity in terms of contents and design creates its very own approach to the subject of silence.

T: Sounds of Silence
D: desres design group
C: Petra Eichler,
   Susanne Kessler
W: Artist exhibition
   catalog
L: German
Y: 2007

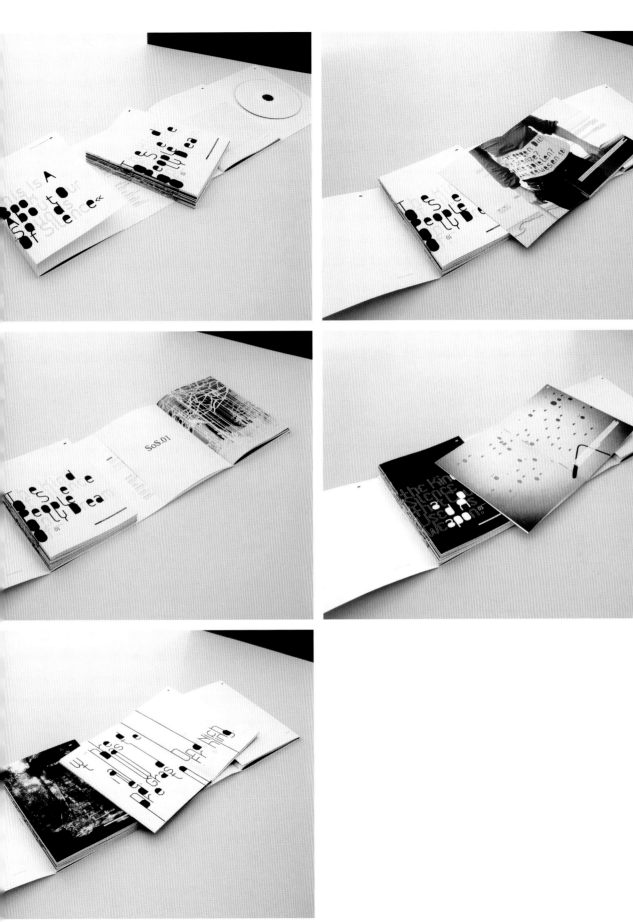

'Sleeve'

Detroit Underground, generic sleeve concept, design and typography by Gandl, 2004. A graphical pattern system derived from world maps was used to define a release index which also matches perfectly with a map of Detroit masked by Gandl's typeface NBForm™, a typeface he originally designed for the Typography issue (196) of the European Design Magazine 'form.' The customer receives a free copy of the typeface with the purchase of the record.

T: Detroit Underground
   Generic Sleeve
D: Neubau
   (NeubauBerlin.com)
C: Detroit Underground
W: Record sleeve
L: English
Y: 2004

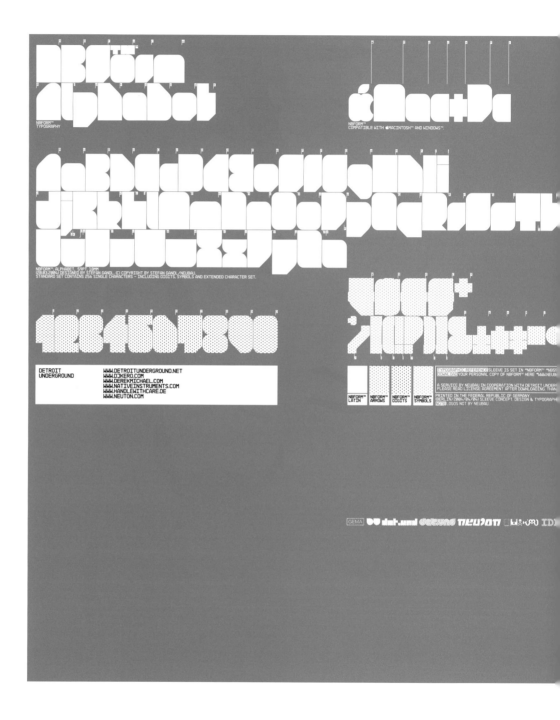

DETROIT UNDERGROUND

"DET.UND GENERIC SLEEVE "LOOK INSIDE FOR RELEASE INFO. ""WW.DETROIT UNDERGROUND.NET

DETROIT
UNDERGROUND | SCALE
1:500.000 | BAR CODE
(SEE VINYL LABEL)

(GEN. SLEEVE)
RELEASE INDEX

| R:01 | R:02 | R:03 | R:04 | R:05 | R:06 | R:07 | R:08 | R:09 | R:10 |

LOOK INSIDE
FOR FURTHER RELEASE DETAILS

RELEASE
REFERENCE

DETROIT
UNDERGROUND

WWW.DETROITUNDERGROUND.NET
WWW.DKHERDZPANEL.COM
WWW.DERMATINSTRUMENTS.COM
WWW.DATTLEINSTRUMENTS.COM
WWW.NUMA.ILSTHEARE.DE
WWW.NEUTON.COM

'Space'

'Re' means reproduce
like recycling or
regeneration. The
typography on the wall
surfaces means that a
green life is repro-
duced on the surface
of concrete walls when
it is viewed from a
regular place. The
typography is designed
on the wall surface so
as to materialize 2-
dimensional typography
in 3-dimensional space.

T:Re
D:KOKOKUMARU,Co Ltd.
C:Osaka University
   of Art
W:Environment/space
L:English
Y:2003

'Square'

Type treatment for a band. square-extension is an audio-visual band based in Poland. It is a multidisciplinary project that expresses its beliefs and ideas via the medium of music, video, graphics and text.

T:square-extension
D:mylifesupport™
C:square-extension
W:Commercial
L:English
Y:2007

'Sports'

Typographic designs for
shop display units. The
designs are printed in
gold on white leather.

T:Revolution/Destiny
D:Non-format
C:Nike
W:Shop display
L:English
Y:2005

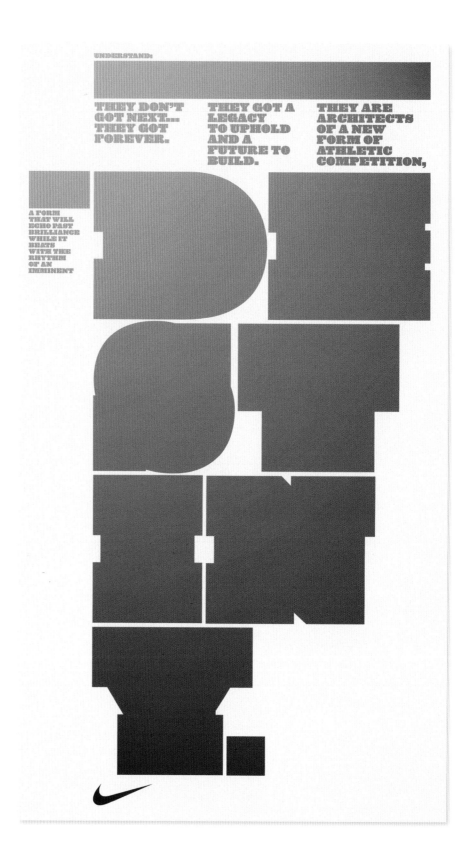

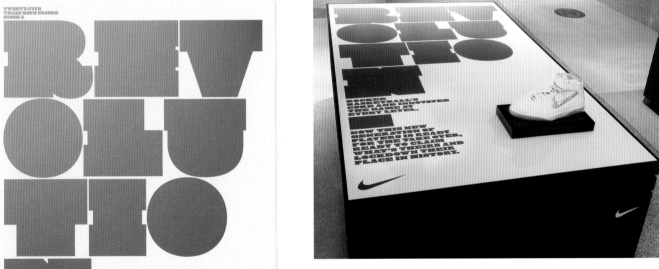

TWENTY-FIVE
YEARS HAVE PASSED
SINCE A

REVOLUTION

ROCKED
BASKETBALL'S
CORE AND INNOVATED
THE GAME AT
EVERY LEVEL.

NOW THIS NEW
GENERATION OF
PLAYERS IS READY
FOR THE TAKE OVER,
READY TO CLAIM
WHAT'S THEIRS AND
LOCKDOWN THEIR
PLACE IN HISTORY.

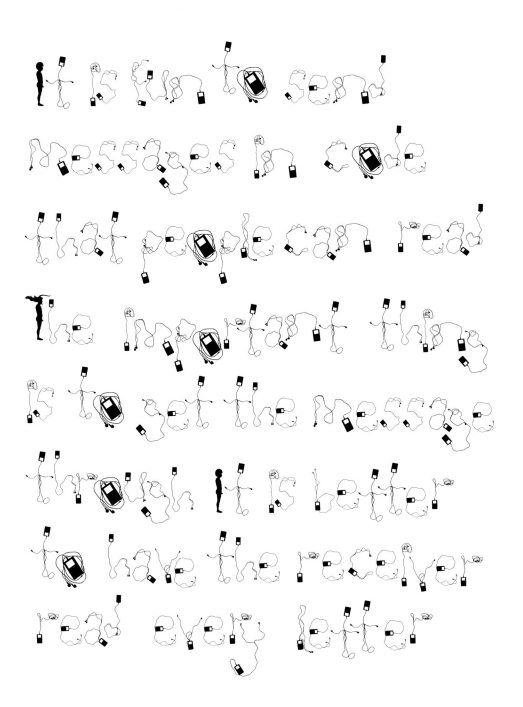

It is fun to send messages in code that people can read the important thing is to get the message through it is better to have the receiver read every letter

'Stereotype'

iType is a 'stereotype' that was designed from a desire to embed metaphor, mythology, popular culture, and innuendo into a typeface. The alphabet was made on the occasion of Post Typography's call for experimental typography, and it is now part of 'Alphabet: An Exhibition of Hand-Drawn Lettering and Experimental Typography,' travelling throughout the United States and abroad.

T: iType
D: Topos Graphics
C: Topos Graphics
W: Typeface
L: English
Y: 2005

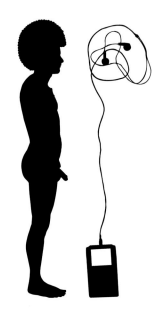

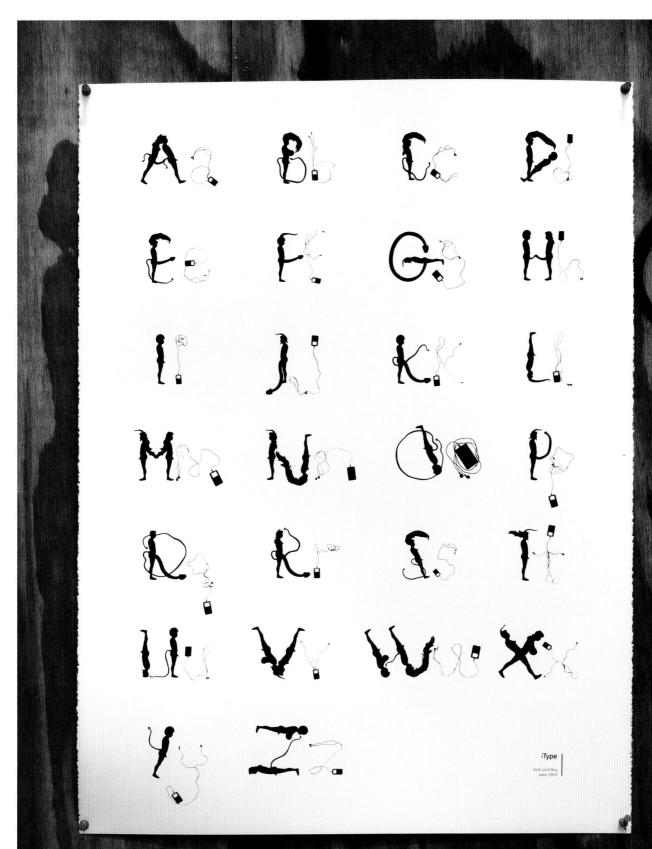

'Stick'

NBStick™ is a typeface that was exclusively produced for the German design and fashion magazine called Jpeople. NBStick™ is inspired by the work of Markus Dressen.

T:NBStick™
D:Neubau
  (NeubauBerlin.Com)
C:Jpeople Magazine
  Germany
W:Illustration
L:English
Y:2004

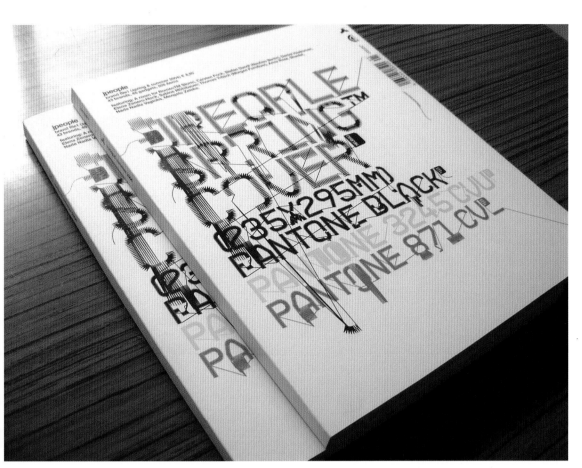

'Still-life'

It is made for New Year's Eve as Serial Cut™ wanted to wish everyone a happy new year. Together with the release of the newsletter titled 'Colour&Illusion for 2007,' the poster is made with huge real 3-dimensional words (props) in different colours. It was real still-life photography with a guy moving the scenes.

T: Fan Poster
D: Serial Cut™
C: Serial Cut™
W: Promotion
L: English
Y: 2006

'Structure'

To place artwork in
the windows of a shop,
Jo intented to create
some new typographic
illustration. As
the space was quite
deep on one side it
seemed it would be
more interesting to
create a 3-dimensional
interpretation of the
designer's typographic
work. With the help
of set builder Tony
Hornecker who built
the structures in wood
from Jo's drawings,
the project worked out
really well.

T: B-Store Letters
D: Jo Ratcliffe
C: B-Store, UK
W: 3D installation
L: English
Y: 2006

  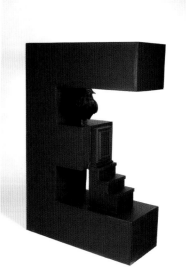

'Toy'

They look like simple
English characters
blocks at first. By
combining the parts,
they will transform
into Kanji or English
characters with the
same meaning. You can
also freely make unique
shapes or discover new
combinations.

T: TOYPOGRAPHY
D: Dainippon Type
   Organization
W: Toy
C: KOKUYO
L: English, Japanese
Y: 2007

HORSE

MONKEY

RABBIT

BIRD 鳥

FISH 魚

BEAR 熊

'Tubular'

5 posters using Lorem Ipsum Dolor Sit Amet, fake text. The idea behind is just to make a visual exercise around type, content and concept was not a priority in this project. Designers consume just shapes and images but not content, here designers use only a fake text to express 5 different tubular letters.

T:Lorem Ipsum Series
D:Alex Trochut
C:Alex Trochut
W:Poster
Y:2007

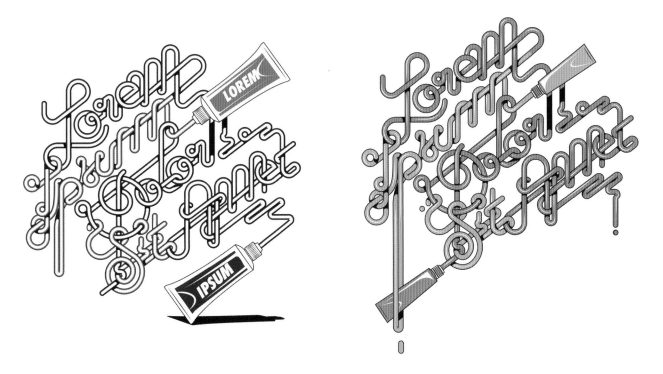

'Univers'

NBUnivers™ is a
computer-programmed
typeface that was
designed for the
NBUnivers project.
NBUnivers™ contains
255 characters (upper
case only).

T:NBUnivers™
D:Neubau
   (NeubauBerlin.Com)
C:NeubauLaden.com
W:Illustration
Y:2004

'Vågen våkner!'

Poster and identity made for the music and art festival 'Vågen våkner!.' The festival took place at Vågsall-menningen in Bergen in the early summer. None of the designers had ever been to the place before, but to them it sounded like a vicious animal. The poster was made with green leaves that had just sprung out on trees in order to keep the feel of summer, it seemed like a good idea to try out leaves and vegetables for the heading. The leek was particularly good. The leaves were highlighted with spot varnish.

T:Vågen våkner
D:Yokoland
C:Vågen våkner
W:Poster, Identity
L:Norwegian
Y:2005

'Villa'

Poster for a live night
held by Metronomicon
Audio at The Villa in
Oslo. The poster was
made with collage,
and combined several
different types of
handmade letters.

T:Metronomicon Audio at
  The Villa
D:Yokoland
C:Metronomicon Audio /
  The Villa
W:Poster
L:Norwegian
Y:2007

'Virtual'

Tybrid – Oded Ezer's
typo hybrids is a new
work created specially
for an invitational
poster exhibition
themed 'My favorite
Game' that was held in
July 2007 in Ithaca,
and in September
in Athens, Greece.
'Tybrid' consists of
4 squares combined
together, forming
the Hebrew word
'Typography.'

Typography researcher
Yehuda Hofshi
commented, '...
Influenced by
Dadaist methods and
contemporary virtual
hybridizations of
animals and human
beings, Ezer treats
this work as a
suggestion for
typographic/visual
expression, something
to look at and not
necessarily to write
with.'

T: Tybrid (Poster series)
D: Oded Ezer Typography
C: Oded Ezer Typography
P: Oded Ezer
W: Poster
L: Hebrew
M: 50x50cm (each square)
Y: 2007

'Virus'

The brief was to create
spreads with the theme
'...is the public enemy.'
The interpretation took
inspiration by the rising
public awareness of animal
deceases and the danger
in attacks with chemical
weapons. The designers
created a typeface based
on hand drawn sketches of
bacteria and viruses.

T:BD SPREADS
D:Made
P:Peter Dawson
C:Beautiful Decay
W:Fashion graphics
Y:2006

Jessica: DSR tie, OP polo dress, Agent Provocateur Stockings

Michele: Brooklyn Industries shirt and dress, Agent Provocateur Stockings, Pony sneakers

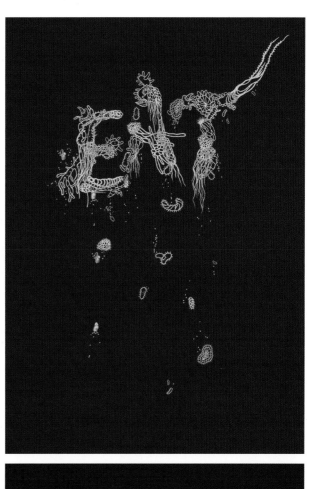

'Wabi-sabi'

Exhibition poster of a book cover that makes tea theme.

The tea of the Chinese character is expressed with the deadwood and it is designed in the image that feels Wabi-sabi.

T:Book cover of Tea
D:Taste Inc.
C:Japan Typography
 Association
W:Custom-made font
L:Japanese
Y:2006

book cover
of tea

ブックカバー展

日時＝2007年1月9日㊋～28日㊐
平日＝午前11：00～午後20：00
日・祝＝午前11：00～午後18：00
場所＝美鈴堂（みすずどう）
※入場無料・月曜日定休
※初日＝午後18：00～20：00
オープニングパーティ開催
www.misuzudo-b.com

[Book Cover Exhibition (Book of Tea)] Design by Taetsuya Naitsu

'War'

The pronunciation of a Chinese word '禍' is exactly the same as 'War' in English, thus the designer created a mixed effect of typeface based on that.

T: War
D: Tommy Li design
   Workshop Limited
C: NO WAR
W: Poster
L: Chinese
Y: 2003

'Welcome'

Instructions to your own Welcome:

1.Choose an appropriate doorway or step for your Welcome stencil, and lay it in position.

2.Sprinkle chalk dust/ cocoa/dust removed from your vacuum cleaner liberally over the surface.

3.Remove stencil carefully to avoid disturbing dust.

4.Observe as people pass over your Welcome, inadvertently destroying one artwork and creating another.

———————————————

T:Welcome
D:Lizzie Ridout
C:Lizzie Ridout
W:Chalk dust
  intervention
L:English
Y:2002-5

merge of both English
and Chinese typeface.

T:Black & White
D:Tommy Li design
  Workshop Limited
C:Tommy Li Solo
  Exhibition @ ARTtube
   - 'Black & White'
W:Exhibition
L:Chinese, English
Y:2005

是非黑白

李永銓作品展

"Black & White" Works by Tommy Li

地點：地鐵中環站 J 出口 灰岩環接接樓層 | 展覽日期：08-07-2005

Venue : Exit J, Jackson Lobby MTR Central Station, Dates : 08 Jul.

15-08-2005 | 每日中午十二時至晚上八時。查詢電話：2834-6312

- August 2005, 12:00pm — 8:00pm Daily, Enquiry : 2834 6312

ARTtube@mtr
地鐵藝術管道

'Wildlife'

Vault49 has teamed up
with H.Un.T to support
a very worthwhile
animal preservation
cause. The Helping
Understand Taxidermy
society has enlisted
Vault49's services to
promote awareness of
their sterling efforts
in preserving wildlife,
and to disseminate
their charitable motto:
'If you can't save 'em,
stuff 'em.'

T:H.Un.T
D:Vault49
C:Vault49
W:Exhibition
L:English
Y:2007

Invite for Designersblock
in Frankfurt 06 (interior
and furniture show).
Wooden type DB standing
for Designersblock and
DE standing for Germany
fold out to reveal main
information about the
event and floating hot air
balloons. This theme was
continued throughout the
exhibition.

T:Designersblock
  Frankfurt
D:HAWAII DESIGN London
C:Designerblock
W:Exhibition invite
L:English
Y:2006

'X'mas'

Christmas identity
for department store
Selfridges in London.
Park Studio designed
the Selfridges
Christmas 2004 logo.
The brief was to create
a logo which went back
to the essence of
Christmas. The theme
set by Selfridges was
'Christmas Stories.'
The designers took
the idea with their
frequent use of drop
caps and embellished
the letters with
Christmas symbols to
give it a magical,
traditional feel with
a modern and playful
twist. The design
concept was then
applied in-store on
all displays and all
promotional materials.

T: Selfridges Christmas
    Identity
D: Park Studio
C: Selfridges
W: Seasonal identity,
    Retail graphic
L: English
Y: 2004

'Yellow'

Branding for D&AD
Global Awards
Nominations Exhibition
2007.

T: D&AD Global Awards
   Nominations Exhibition
   2007 - Postcard Wallet
D: Build
C: D&AD
W: Print
L: English
Y: 2007

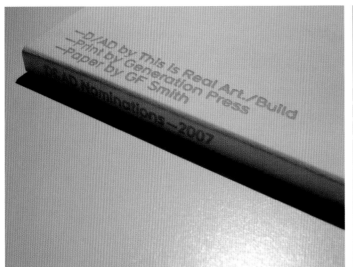

'Zines'

02 is a free contemporary art magazine that issued quaterly. The designers were the artistic directors for 2 years. First the designer created a simple and legible layout. As the iconography was from artists and visual creators, the designers decided to work with a layout that would not interfere with the photos so that there would be no confusion and also decided to create a new alphabet for each issue. The titles are always at the same place, but in different type, each time with a big personality. It is always printed in full black on white paper.

T: 02, contemporary art magazine
D: Sylvia Tournerie
C: 02, contemporary art magazine
W: Editorial
L: English
Y: 2004-6

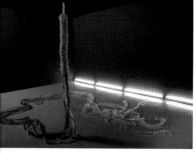

SWEET AND SOUR

par Jill Gasparina

26.dossier

Peut-on être abstrait?

J'aimerais connaître votre méthode.

C'est quoi, être artiste?

LE PERÇU & LE NON-PERÇU* @ PIERRE BISMUTH

par Cécilia Bezzan

Coming soon

JOIE

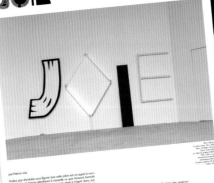

par Patrice Joly

AU TRAVERS DU PRISME

ROBERT SMITHSON

POP MY RELIGION

RÉVÉREND ETHAN ACRES

Interview par Claire Jacquet
Traduction de l'américain par Aude Launay et Claire Jacquet,
avec des éclairages de Mark Alizart.

PRACTICE ZERO TOLERANCE

ADEL ABDESSEMED

par Anne Bonnin

◤ {THS} THOMAS SCHOSTOK DESIGN

Thomas Schostok was born in 1972 and started his career as a salesman for bathroom tiles in 1989. He never studies design because he always thinks that studying design is to be brainwashed. He spent his time working for different design agencies but soon left slavery and founded '{ths}' in 1999, working in his own studio for international and national clients. {ths} has no anger or hate, because it is fondness for Elvis Presley and Barry White records, that is being continuously played during work and thus make him nice and merry. {ths} defines its work as trash urban warfare porn dirt style pop.

Page 046-7

◤ 3 DEEP DESIGN

3 Deep Design is a design and image agency based in Australia with representation in New York, Tokyo and Europe.

3 Deep Design was established in 1996 by Brett Phillips and David Roennfeldt and has since established a reputation of uncompromised design excellence, commitment, passion and design innovation. The 3 Deep group of companies include 3 Deep Design, 3 Deep Publishing and Everything in Between.

3 Deep constantly assembles teams of photographers, illustrators, fashion designers, writers, artists, type foundries, architects and technical developers to realize complex and benchmark projects. 3 Deep's products and services are called upon by the finest bookstores, galleries, private clients and institutions around the world.

Page 158-9, 162-5

◤ ADAM HAYES

Adam Hayes was born in 1981 in Stoke-on-Trent, England. After graduating from the Royal College of Art in 2006 he began working from his desk in East London on projects for himself, his friends and clients worldwide.

A great lover of the outdoors, Adam often enjoys fell walking, mountain biking and camping in the UK's beautiful countryside. This is reflected in his work where his designs are founded upon hand drawn and organic forms that mix with his interests in typography and language.

Page 141

◤ ALEX TROCHUT

Alex Trochut was born and lived in Barcelona. He loves drawing and he spent hours in drawing when he was a child.

Alex studied in Elisava, Barcelona and had worked with Alexander Branczyk at Xplicit and Moniteurs. After 2 years working in Toormix, Alex joined Vasava. Right now Alex is freelancing for clients from London, New York, Amsterdam etc. and projects like Nike, Coke as well as some small projects. Alex has been working for companies like Non-format or Weiden and Kennedy as a freelance.

Page 202-3

◤ ANDREW BYROM

Andrew Byrom was born in Liverpool, England. In 1997 he opened his own studio in London designing for various clients including Penguin Books, The British Academy of Composers and Songwriters and The Guardian Newspaper.

Byrom moved to America in 2000. He now divides his time between teaching, designing and playing with his sons Louis and Auden.

His work has featured in design magazines like Print, Creative Review and Architectural Record; and books including AIGA Annual 2003, G1: New Dimensions in Graphic Design, American Corporate Identity 22 and New Typographic Design.

His type designs have been exhibited across the US including The National Design Centre in New York and he has been recognized with a Certificate of Excellence from the American Institute of Graphic Arts.

Page 068-9, 89, 124-7, 154-5

◤ APIRAT INFAHSAENG

Apirat is a 25 year-old visual artist and designer working in New York City. He is an incessant form maker and experimenter with a fondness for plaid, video games, music, science fiction, and trying to play the drums. Apirat is constantly absorbed in projects; self-initiated, collaborative, and client-driven, and is a participating designer at Ogilvy&Mather's BIG (Brand Innovation Group) in NYC. He lives in Brooklyn with his girlfriend and 3 cats.

ARTLESS INC.

artless is a design group based in Tokyo. Active in the field of visual communication, the unit's broad activities include CI, branding, graphics and product design, interactive installations, space production and video. In addition to client-driven projects, the unit places great importance on its own original works, and has produced both graphic and interactive art, as well as having its distinctive works published and exhibited in various places. Although based in Tokyo, their activities are not limited only to Japan, they also participate in projects overseas.

ARTROOM - COMMERCIAL RADIO PRODUCTIONS LTD.

In the little Artroom under the Commercial Radio Productions Ltd., 6 fiery designers give themselves in the designs of the Radio (FM881 and FM903) as well as related parties. From 2-dimensional graphic designs, huge settings and stage designs for events and concerts, to miscellaneous designs like events props, stickers and signage, endless design verve makes Artroom@CRP an unforgettable place to create.

ATELIER TÉLESCOPIQUE

Stéphane Meurice, Sébastien Delobel, Xavier Meurice, Guillaume Berry and Baptiste Servais are the creative brains behind Atelier télescopique and its companion type foundry, AinsFont. This close-knit team of designers, based in Lille - France, opened its studio in 1998.

Along with their groundbreaking work in multiple media - print, video, web and art exhibitions, they also create unique typefaces. This eclecticism can be found in their clientele, which is composed of big industries and institutions as well as members of the culture scene.

BUILD

Build is a graphic design studio which prides itself on its craft-like approach to print. It was founded in 2001 by Michael C. Place and Nicky Place, and has since established itself as a studio with an almost obsessive attention to detail.

Build is Michael, Nicky, Brockmann and Betty.

Build. Print With Love.

BYGGSTUDIO

Byggstudio works with a combination of self-initiated projects and commercial work focusing on graphic design and illustration. The designers see graphic design as a way to communicate ideas beyond visual expression where strong aesthetics, colours and humour play an important part. Recently they have been developing graphic profiles, exhibition design, posters, typography, web design and editorial magazine work in Scandinavia specializing in photographic illustration. Byggstudio was founded in 2006 by Hanna Nilsson, Markus Bergström and Sofia Østerhus.

CLAIRE SCULLY

Studied BA Graphic and Media design at London College of Communication (2001-4) and Central Saint Martins (2004-6) for MA Communication Design, as well as continually working on many personal projects and frequently collaborating with various artists, London-based Claire works works as a freelance illustrator.

The Quiet Revolution is the body of work by Claire inspired by the conflicting and harmonious relationships the urban environment has with the natural world. With a mix of playful humour with sinister undertones of conflict and mutation, the Quiet Revolution is a visual exploration into the relationship between the natural world and the urban environment. The illustator shows the significance of nature within a cities' surroundings and the struggle for power human has with it by using a combination of printed illustrations with moving image.

CODESIGN LTD

Hung Lam established CoDesign Ltd with Eddy Yu in 2003. Lam has been actively participating in international design, cultural and art projects. He has won a number of prominent design awards during his career advancement.

Recent years, Lam has extended his creativity and vision from graphic design across media and has participated in various exhibitions and installation shows.

CONOR & DAVID

Conor Nolan and David Wall are designers working on print and interactive projects in Dublin, Ireland.

CORP.UNIT

Corp.Unit started off in early 1999 with the simple plan in mind - operating as a design studio that navigates disciplines in graphic design, web design, product design, film and music for the greater good. Corp.Unit collaborates with different talented artists in order to handle a variety of small to big projects. Strongly following the notion that things can always be approached and done differently, Corp.Unit tries to explore the untouchable, alter the recognizable and create the irresistible in order to communicate ideas and solve problems.

DAINIPPON TYPE ORGANIZATION

An experimental typographic team that established in 1993. From the Japanese to English alphabet, the designers deconstruct, shape, and form fresh typography that without the lost of irresistible Japanese feel. Their work is available as font packages and motion graphics.

DAVID LANE

David Lane graduated from BA Graphic Design at St Martins. He then went on to freelance and worked for Multistorey and Wolff Olins. He has created record covers for Bands such as Gossip and the Noisettes, and worked on projects such as the London 2012 Olympic logo. He now works from his own studio in East London.

DESRES DESIGN GROUP

desres is a design and consultancy studio and is active in a wide range of projects across a growing variety of media. desres projects feature concept, design, illustration, interactive design, typography, and art direction along with experience in film, installation and moving image. desres works for corporate, cultural and private clients as well as advertising and event agencies. desres also engages in collaboration with other companies and professionals.

desres is based in Frankfurt Main.

FROMKTOJ/FROMJTOK

FromKtoJ/FromJtoK is a growing and often frazzled workshop organized around JK Keller and Keetra Dean Dixon. The duos push their focus towards non-commissioned work, but occasionally find the lure of a shiny client job too seductive to resist. Voted most likely to meander, JK & KDD straddle a wide set of mediums in the pursuit of 2D & 3D projects. A vow to follow their obsession keeps the two running endlessly on new paths. Most recent obsession: the prolific power of computation!

GGGRAFIK

With Niklaus Troxler as his diploma mentor and a degree in Communication Design from the Darmstadt University of Applied Sciences in his pocket, Götz Gramlich formed gggrafik in 2005.

Besides working for major clients and agencies in Germany and Switzerland, Gramlich has earned international critical acclaim for his poster designs – both for commercial and non-profit purposes – and magazine covers. Bold, fearless and universal in their graphic vocabulary, Gramlich's designs speak an easy-to-understand, eye-

catching language that can be termed iconographic in its simplicity and impact of message.

GRANDPEOPLE

Grandpeople is a Norwegian design studio. It is run by Magnus Voll Mathiassen, Magnus Helgesen and Christian Bergheim who met at art school where they started to work together. Grandpeople has been a full-time studio since 2005. They work with small and large clients in the fields of advertising, art, fashion, music and exhibitions mostly. Dedicated and haunted by their preferences.

GUY HAVIV

After a few years working as a software developer, Guy thought computer science might be too boring and finally went on to pursue interest in graphics (and mostly, interactive) design and went to design school. The designer fell in love with typography and print.

GYÖNGY LAKY

Gyöngy Laky, (b. Budapest, Hungary 1944) is a sculptor. Her work is exhibited widely both in the US and abroad and is in many permanent museum collections. Laky studied at University of California, Berkeley, and was a professor at UC, Davis, until retirement in 2005. A past recipient of a National Endowment for the Arts Fellowship, she was also commissioned by the US Federal Art-in-Architecture Program. In 2003 a book about her work, 'Portfolio Series: Gyöngy Laky,' was published and UC, Berkeley, released her oral history. The Smithsonian Institution maintains a collection of Laky's personal papers at the Archives of American Art.

HAMLET AU-YEUNG

Hamlet graduated from the Hong Kong Art School in 2007 and currently works as a graphic designer in 84000 communications.

HAWAII DESIGN LONDON

HAWAII is a London based design/illustration agency set up by Paul Mcanelly. The aim of the studio is to stay small and build a close relationship with each client.

The studio has a diverse mix of clients to date including, MTV Europe, BFI, Arts Council, Gap Europe and Universal Music.

HJÄRTA SMÄRTA

Hjärta Smärta works with graphic design and illustration since 2001. The designers live and work in Stockholm, Sweden.

ICELAND ACADEMY OF THE ARTS, GRAPHIC DESIGN GRADUATION CLASS OF 2006

The group is the graduation class of 2006 in graphic design, studying at the Iceland Academy of the Arts.

JO RATCLIFFE

Jo Ratcliffe works with illustration, typography and set design. Her work has been featured internationally in publications such as the Guardian, British Vogue, Vogue Nippon, Dazed and Confused, Another Magazine, Carlos and GQ.

She has been involved in working on branding and advertising projects for companies including Rimmel, Orange, Sony and MTV.

Other work includes illustration for t-shirts, album covers, comics, books and exhibitions working with Channel 4, Stussy, Levis and more.

Jo lives and works in London.

KHAKI CREATIVE & DESIGN, INC.

Born and raised in Northeastern China, Nod gave up his factory job and moved to Beijing to pursue his dream in incorporating art into his life.

Today Nod is the creative director and co-founder of his own creative group, Khaki Creative & Design. Home-based in Beijing, Khaki Creative & Design focuses on creative brand-

...services for clients in China, US and UK as they look to explore the rest of the world.

Nod's personal works have been displayed in exhibitions in the UK, Germany, Japan, Mainland China and Taiwan.

◤ KOKOKUMARU,CO LTD.

Yoshimaru Takahashi is the visiting professor of Osaka University of Art Graduate school and the superintendent of KOKOKUMARU,Co Ltd. with numerous awards like the Silver Award at New York Art Directors Club and the Best Work at Japan Typography Association Annual. Yoshimaru is a member of the Japan Graphic Designers Association Inc., Japan Typography Association Inc., Tokyo Typo Directors Club and New York Type Directors Club.

◤ LIZZIE RIDOUT

Lizzie tends to avoid working in one particular discipline, believing the form of any outcome should be suggested by the theme or idea at its heart. The majority of Lizzie's work stems from the desire to discover: a fact, a story, an object, an image, a ritual, a process, a history. These discoveries then inspire projects that borrow working methods from graphic design, fine art and illustration.

The designer graduated from the Royal College of Art in 2002 and has since been involved in various commissioned and self-initiated projects. Lizzie has exhibited nationally and internationally and lecture in graphics at universities across the UK.

◤ MADE

Made is a multi-disciplinary design studio based in Oslo, Norway. They can be found far up in the mountains, in the middle of the fjords or deep in the forest. Made was established in 2004/5 by 3 partners, and constantly grows. Made works with a diverse range of projects, and believes in the strength of a good idea. The client list is impressive, di-

... vice and Jo as the work pro duced. Made is part of the worldwide TBWA group.

◤ MANUEL KIEM

Born in 1981 in Silandro, Italy, Manuel Kiem studies Graphic Design at the University of Applied Arts Vienna. Since 2003 he also works as a freelance graphic designer in Vienna and Berlin.

◤ MICHAEL PERRY

Michael Perry runs a small design studio in Brooklyn, New York, working with clients like MTV, Brooklyn Industries, Dwell Magazine, New York Times Magazine and so many more. Perry just finished his first book titled 'Hand Job' published by Princeton Architectural Press that will be on book shelf near fall 2007. Doodling away night and day, Perry creates new typefaces and sundry graphics that inevitably evolve into his new work, exercising the great belief that the generation of piles is the sincerest form of creative process. He has shown his work around the world, from the booming metropolis of London to Los Angeles to the homegrown expanses of Kansas.

◤ MILKXHAKE

Milkxhake is a young Hong Kong-based design unit co-founded by graphic designer Javin Mo and interactive designer Wilson Tang in 2002, mainly focuses on graphic and interactive mixtures. In 2004, Javin was invited to join FABRICA, the Benetton Research and Communication Center in Italy. In 2005, he re-initiated Milkxhake with Wilson as one of the most energetic design collective based in Hong Kong. Their works have been selected by Tokyo Type Directors Club Awards (2004/6) and Hong Kong Designers Association Awards (2005/7). In 2006, Javin was awarded as the Young Gun 5 from the New York ADC. In 2007, they also received merit from 86th New York ADC and British D&AD Awards. Their works have been widely published in international design magazines and journals.

◤ MISPRINTED TYPE

Eduardo Recife is an artist/illustrator and designer from Brazil. You can check some of his works on www.misprintedtype.com.

◤ MYLIFESUPPORT™

Michael Kosmicki is a 21-year-old aspiring designer from London. Born and raised in Poland, Mike has moved to London 5 years ago where he has been studying and working as a freelance designer. He usually operates under the names of mylifesupport™ and hoodlumbranding. In 2006 after years of printing t-shirts for his friends, he has started a small t-shirt label called RFUTM. Mike is obsessed with sneakers, coffee, skulls, typography and jazz music.

◤ NB: STUDIO

Established in 1997 by 3 passionate, creative and highly motivated designers Alan Dye, Nick Finney and Ben Stott, NB Studio is an award-winning design consultancy with reputation for simplicity and clarity of communication. They do not follow trends. Inspired by new challenges, problem solving, and tea and biscuits, their approach to design has enabled them to build strong relationships with clients including Knoll, Land Securities, Mothercare, and the Tate.

◤ NEUBAU (NEUBAUBERLIN.COM)

Neubau was founded by Stefan Gandl in 2001. It works in the fields of screen design, print & video design and typography. Gandl's work is published in countless international publications. In 2005 Neubau released the bestselling book 'Neubau Welt' which is followed by 'Neubau Modul' in 2007. Since 2006 Neubau is Stefan Gandl and Christoph Grünberger.

http://www.NeubauBerlin.Com
http://www.NeubauLaden.Com

NOA BEMBIBRE

Noa was born in A Coruña, Spain in 1981. The designer lives and works in Helsinki, Finland since 2002. Being graduated from MA Fine Arts in the Basque Country University and MA Applied Art and Design in the University of Art and Design Helsinki, Noa worked as freelance for different companies and creative studios from 2003-6 and established own company Noa Bembibre Oy Ltd in the year 2005. Noa is now a graphic designer of Design Studio Muotohiomo in Helsinki. The designer's work 'Cats Let Nothing Darken Their Roar' gained Honorable Mention Vuoden Huiput 2005 (Anual advertising and graphic design prizes in Finland).

NON-FORMAT

Non-Format is a creative team comprising Kjell Ekhorn (Norwegian) and Jon Forss (British). They work on a range of projects including art direction, design and illustration for music industry, arts and culture, fashion and advertising clients. They also art direct Varoom — the journal of illustration and made images.

ODED EZER TYPOGRAPHY

Oded Ezer is an Israeli typographer, type designer, typo experimentalist and design educator.

Graduated at the V.C.D dep. of the Bezalel Academy, Jerusalem, Ezer founded his own independent studio in Tel Aviv, Israel in the year 2000, specializing in typographic aspects of branding and publication designs.

As a member of the DCI (Designers Community of Israel), Ezer teaches in several academies in Israel, among which the Shenkar College of Design, one of the most distinguished design academies in Israel.

While constantly working as a commercial designer, Ezer runs experimental typo art projects, where he explores non-conventional solutions in Hebrew and Latin typography.

PARK STUDIO

Park Studio is a London-based graphic design studio founded by Linda Lundin and Nina Nägel in 2002. Park Studio is the place to come to if you want a solution which is friendly but sharp, challenging and always on brand, whether it is for an identity, publications, retail or exhibition graphics. Park Studio works with a wide range of clients from the Design Museum and the British Council to Selfridges and Oasis.

PAULO GARCIA/LODMA. LOCATION DOESN'T MATTER ANYMORE

Lodma. Location Doesn't Matter Anymore was founded by Paulo Garcia in 2005. The studio is dedicated to innovative thinking across a wide range of different media, such as motion graphics, print, identity, brand consulting, interactive, illustration and experimental work.

PLEASELETMEDESIGN

pleaseletmedesign (PLMD) is a duo of young graphic designers comprising Pierre Smeets (b. 1981) and Damien Aresta (b. 1979). They set up their own small design studio in 2004 after graduating from Saint-Luc Higher School of Arts in Liège, Belgium and spending almost a full year in ERG (Graphic Research School) in Brussels, Belgium.

The projects of pleaseletmedesign range from graphic design, books, posters, identities and stationery to exhibition design, signage, titles sequences, website and everything else in cultural sectors as diverse as music, architecture, cinema and advertising clients. PLMD is based in Brussels, Belgium.

POST TYPOGRAPHY

Originally conceived and founded in 2001 as an avant garde anti-design movement by Nolen Strals and Bruce Willen, Post Typography specializes in graphic design, conceptual typography, and custom lettering/illustration with additional forays into art, apparel, music, curatorial work, design theory and vandalism. Their work has received numerous fancy design awards and has been featured in publications such as Ellen Lupton's Thinking With Type and D.I.Y.: Design It Yourself, The Art of Modern Rock, STEP Magazine, Metropolis magazine, and Taschen's Contemporary Graphic Design. Post Typography has appeared in multiple design and art exhibitions, and their posters are collected by high school punk rockers and prominent designers, whom they consider equally important. Strals and Willen currently teach classes in design and typography at the Maryland Institute College of Art, and have lectured at the Cooper Union, Minneapolis College of Art & Design, and Harvard University among others.

R2 DESIGN

Lizá Defossez Ramalho and Artur Rebelo founded the R2 design studio in Oporto, where they have since undertaken projects in the field of visual communication design, mainly for contemporary art, architecture and theatre.

Since 1996, their work has also included teaching design in various Portuguese colleges and served on various juries, gave lectures and participated in different national and international exhibitions. Their projects have received many awards such as the 'Grand Prix' at the 22nd International Biennale of Graphic Design in Brno and the 'Gold Prize' at the 7th International Poster Triennial of Toyama, Japan in 2003.

ROBERT J.BOLESTA

Graduated from Pratt Institute in May 2007.

SERIAL CUT™

Serial Cut™ is a Madrid based studio that established in 1999 by Sergio del Puerto, licensed in Visual Communication in the UCM (Madrid) and graphic design. The studio works on great variety types of projects although it mainly focuses on the following:

Art Direction - Graphic solutions that aims to provide clients with a special and personal way of communicating their product.

and web projects.

Illustration - A versatile and experimental style based on the 'cut&paste' technique: a mix of vector shapes, photo collage, pixels and pencil strokes. In most cases, typography has a special role to reinforce the idea and generate more impact.

Page 028, 060-1, 065, 112-3, 167-170, 194-5

SI SCOTT DESIGN

Photography is used as one working method rather than separate elements.

Page 139, 148-9

SIGGI ORRI THORHANNESSON

Hordur Larusson, Siggi Orri Thorhannesson and Sol Hrafnsdottir all graduated from The Iceland Academy of the Arts in June 2006 with BA in graphic design. Siggi Orri and Sol are currently working as freelance graphic designers, individually as well as a team while Hordur works both freelance and in a small design studio run by Atli Hilmarsson.

Page 082-3

SIXSTATION

Founded by Benny Luk, a 28-year-old graphic, web, font designer and illustrator. Sixstation is first started as a personal experimental website in 2000. Design style is mainly mixed with modern contemporary and rich traditional Asian culture.

From 2004 to present Benny has changed into a soho style freelancer. He mainly works with international clients such as Nike Asia, MTV Asia and SonyX-Levis etc.

Page 021-3, 080, 134-5, 138, 150-1, 179

STUDIO8 DESIGN

Studio8 Design is an award-winning independent graphic design studio with reputation for delivering intelligent and engaging creative solutions. Based in central London, Studio8 was established in 2005 by Matt Willey and Zoë Bather, formerly Creative Directors at Frost Design London. Working with clients both large and small, in the UK and overseas,

disciplines. With over 15 years of industry experience between them, Matt and Zoë bring a wealth of knowledge and enthusiasm to every new project and offer a scope of capabilities that includes editorial, exhibition, signage, corporate literature, websites and brand identity systems.

Page 012-3

SYLVIA TOURNERIE

Sylvia is working as an independent graphic designer since 1996, especially for music industry and pop rock electro with close collaborations with some bands like Bosco and Mirwais, as well as some independant music labels such as Source. As things went along the designer has been working also for fashion like Levi's, visual identity of AndA (a Japanese brand) and images for Clarks. The art direction of the contemporary art magazine '02' leaded the designer to more typographic work and also logically to the world of art galleries like exhibition posters and catalogues.

Page 084-5, 230-3

TASTE INC.

Born in Osaka, Japan in 1951, Toshiyasu Nanbu graduated from the Osaka High School of Industrial Arts in 1969. He established the Design office Taste Inc. in 1988. Graphic design is believed to be an international language. Nanbu designs based on typography now. The designer won numerous awards like the gold prize of 'The 7th Tokyo Typedirection in Japan' general section in 1995 and the 'HKDA AWARDS 05' in 2005. Nabu is selected by China as the young designer who represents Japan in 2000, and his work collection 'New Generation Graphic Designer/Toshiyasu Nanbu' is published. The one-man show is held in Tokyo designer's space (Roppongi AXIS building).

Page 039, 144, 152, 214-5

TJEP.

Frank Tjepkema and Janneke Hooymans officially joined forces as Tjep. in 2001.

Frank is a Dutch designer based in Amsterdam. He graduated in 1996 from the Design Academy in Eindhoven. Following this he

1998. Frank developed a strong interest in brand related design issues and worked on a variety of projects for well-known brands. He was the head of the design department at the Rietveld Akademie in Amsterdam from 2001 to 2004.

Janneke brings in expertise in the field of interior design and styling. Before joining Tjep., Janneke worked for Neonis, Marcel Wanders and started up her own design company Zus&Zus with Carlijn Kriekaard. Noteworthy projects are: the interior of the Unox Soup Factory and the contribution to the design of the Glasgow Science center.

In 2004 Tjep. won the Dutch Design Awards in the categories interior and fashion design.

Page 106-7

TOMMY LI DESIGN WORKSHOP LIMITED

Tommy Li is Hong Kong's master designer in this generation renowned for his 'Black Humour' and 'Audacious Visual' designs. Spanning Hong Kong, China, Macau and Japan, he is one of a few designers to have penetrated the international market.

Over the years, Tommy received almost 500 awards. His most distinct achievement to date has been record owner to 4 awards from New York Directors' Club, which honours outstanding results among Chinese designers.

Page 216, 218-221

TOPOS GRAPHICS

Topos Graphics calls home the place where thought and form meet, and they live and work with graphics in New York City. Specializing in ideas for print, they are interested in projects that both raise questions and point towards answers. Small or large in scale and intimate or public in sentiment, their work is propelled by a desire to see words and images actively participate across multiple platforms. Led by Seth Labenz and Roy Rub, their doors have been open for business going on one year.

Page 077, 190-1

TSANG KIN-WAH

Graduated from the Chinese University of Hong Kong in 2000, Tsang Kin-wah received his master degree from Camberwell College of Arts, the London Institute in 2003.

Tsang's works mainly focus on investigating the specific meanings created by combining the swear words with the elegant image and by presenting this as a form of wallpaper, he specifically create different installation works for different sites and venues. Among these years, he has taken part in various group exhibitions in Europe and Asia, and has his solo exhibitions in various cities like Tokyo, Barcelona, Madrid, etc.

Tsang has received awards likes Tokyo TDC Prize 2007, 2005 Sovereign Asian Art Prize, Prize of Excellence - Hong Kong Art Biennial 2001, etc. His works are collected by Sovereign Art Foundation, Museum of Design Zurich (Switzerland), Shu Uemura (Costa Mesa, California), etc.

Page 122-3

VAULT49

Graduating together from the London College of Printing, Jonathan Kenyon and John Glasgow launched Vault49 alongside their final year degree show. The collaboration quickly emerged as one of the UK's leading and most innovative design companies with a broad portfolio spanning typography, illustration, photography and web design.

Following their relocation to New York in 2004, Vault49 continue to achieve sustained coverage in the best of the UK, US, and worldwide design press by virtue of the breadth of their ability across all fields of design, and reputation for creating consistently innovative work for an international client list.

Page 222

WHAA

Whaa are 3 independent graphic designers graduated from the University of Arts of Lausanne Ecal (Switzerland) in Visual Communication, Graphic Design in 2006. They decided to create Whaa in order to share their skills and interests. Illustration, photography, experimental typography, book layout and animated gif are their media choices. Please visit www.whaa.ch, they love fan mail.

All work designed by ecal/ visual communication graphic design/design student/David Stettler, Lyne Friederich or Florence Tétier

Page 011, 146-7

WIDMEST

Widmest is Eric Ellis, a Chicago based designer. When he is not colouring or playing with blocks he likes to make big posters.

Page 090-1

WILL PERRENS

Graphic designer based in London.

Page 044, 070-1

WYETH HANSEN

Wyeth is a freelance designer and artist based out of Brooklyn, working in video, audio, and printed material.

Born and raised in the armpit of California and relocated to the northeast, Wyeth's work is a blend of west coast vibes and east coast rigor. This mix is evident in his work, which oscillates between geometric minimalizm and psychedelic naturalizm, yet which remains somehow unified.

Wyeth has exhibited work on both coasts and across the pond; clients include MTV, Vh1, the AIGA, Sundance, 2K by Gingham, Ghostly Records Intl., and a legion of design studios throughout the city and various publications.

Page 051

YOKOLAND

Yokoland is a graphic design and illustration studio that was started by Espen Friberg and Aslak Gurholt Rønsen sometime between their graduation from High School in 2000 and from The National Academy of the Arts, Oslo in 2004/2005. In the beginning there was no intention that Yokoland would be a graphic design studio (it sorted to happen along the way). Yokoland was just the place to experiment various small projects. In 2006 the studio grew, and Thomas Tengesdal Nordby became the third inhabitant of the country. Yokoland also run the record label Metronomicon Audio together with the label's musicians, and have been doing all the design for the label since 2002. Yokoland is based in Oslo, Norway. A monograph about the studio, 'Yokoland - As we go up we go down,' was published by Die Gestalten Verlag in 2006.

Page 206-7

ZION GRAPHICS

Zion Graphics is a multifaceted design agency based in Stockholm, Sweden. Founded by Ricky Tillblad in 2002, Zion's work crosses over vast disciplines including corporate identity, fashion, interactive media, packaging and print. Their clients are J. Lindeberg, Adidas, Sony BMG, Universal Music, EMI Music, Pee&Poo, Peak Performance and more.

Page 038